The I Hate My Job Handbook

THE

I HATE
MY JOB
HANDBOOK

HOW TO DEAL WITH HELL AT WORK

Ellen Tien and Valerie Frankel

FAWCETT COLUMBINE • NEW YORK

A Fawcett Columbine Book
Published by Ballantine Books

LIBRARY OF CONGRESS CATALOG CARD NUMBER: 94-90900

ISBN: 0-449-90886-0

Cover illustration by Bonnie Timmons

Manufactured in the United States of America
First Edition: January 1996
10 9 8 7 6 5 4 3 2

To all the women who
made it work.

WITHDRAWN

Contents

Acknowledgments   ix

1: The Beginning of the End   3

2: Your Fearful Leader   22

3: Work/Counterwork   44

4: The Body Politic   69

5: Nightmare on Work Street   97

6: Misery: Your Top Ten Questions   115

7: Should I Stay or Should I Go?   140

8: Playing with Fire   157

9: Let Freedom Ring   177

10: Sweet Revenge   200

Acknowledgments

Thanks to Julia, Chi, and Anita Tien, and Judy, Howie, and Alison Frankel, for always seeing us through; Julie Merberg for a great start; Sherri Rifkin for making the Rifkin Account a done deal; Loretta Fidel for backing us up; Debra Wise for living up to her name; Carol, Colette, Ellen W., Howie, Jeanie, Judy M., Kathy, and Rebecca for helping us out; Helen, Guy, Michelle, Gabé, and Elizabeth for proving that good bosses do exist; Frank Rosenberg for the incentive; Glenn Rosenberg for his infinite patience; Will Dana for feeding, reading, and being an all-around good-humor man; and finally, to dear, morsely, cat's-meow-ly Marshall Sella for his sharp pencil, mind, and wit.

And special thanks to all our sources. Your secrets are safe with us.

The I Hate My Job Handbook

1

The Beginning of the End

Sunday night, 11:59 P.M. You're lying in bed, staring at the ceiling. You've been tossing and turning for hours—what time is it, anyway? You sneak a peek at your digital clock: eleven fifty-nine. Great. One more minute until the harshest day of the week. Five more days until next weekend. Six more months until you get vacation . . . Two more weeks until your period . . . Three blind mice, see how they . . .

And then you wake up. Gosh, you must've drifted off for a second there. You roll over to check the time: nine-fourteen. Nine-fourteen? NINE-FOURTEEN??? FIFTEEN MORE MINUTES UNTIL YOU HAVE TO BE IN THE OFFICE. What happened to the alarm? *While you were sleeping, someone turned off the wake-up-to-music*. Just like last Monday. And the Monday before. What is with this pattern? You throw the covers on the floor. Late again—your backstabbing coworkers will have a field day. Your boss will have a hissy fit. You wonder if you need to shower. You wonder if you should wash your hair. As you frantically brush your teeth, and mentally put together an outfit, you settle on hower, no shair. Make that shower, no hair.

Welcome to the working week. We're glad you could drag yourself out of bed to join the legions of perfectly healthy people who contemplated calling in sick, too. As someone once said (we think it was Aesop, but maybe it was Martha Stewart), misery loves company. And god knows, your company breeds misery.

Although hating a job isn't the worst thing that's ever going to happen to you, studies show it ranks somewhere between hair loss and death. Translation: It's bad. Still, while you may feel like you're hurtling uncontrollably into the unemployment abyss, there's actually a method to this madness. You see, the road from Hating-a-Job to Needing-a-Job is rife with warning signs. We know. We've driven right past them. As such, in our never-ending quest to make your lives easier, we've backtracked and discovered—with the help of two or three (hundred) of our closest associates—that there are five emotional pit stops along the career collision course. You might pull in at all of them, or you may only visit one or two. Either way, study them carefully: If you know the terrain, you'll be better equipped to travel defensively. So, forget the Rogaine, unplug the Dr. Kevorkian blue-plate special—and get ready to roll.

1. Obsession Point

Everyone fixates on his or her job to some degree: What with spending forty hours a week or more with the same people in the same place, you'd have to be the Dalai Lama not to dish. The danger lies in getting hung up on the details. When the going gets tough, the tough can get obsessive—suddenly, every tiny thing requires hours of analysis. Taken to extremes, this total absorption has the potential to wipe you out completely. "Obsession is sometimes a coping device," says Marilyn Puder-York, Ph.D., a clinical psychologist in New York City who specializes in executive therapy. "If you're concentrating on problem-solving strategies, you may be productive. But pure fixation—without any thought to solution—is never helpful."

Sarah, a twenty-five-year-old publicist, found this out the hard way. A quick study, she found herself fixating early on. "My first day at work, I knew there would be problems," she says. "It was a small, cliqueish office, and not only was I the outsider, but a good five years younger than everyone else. I thought things would loosen up, but they only got worse. I was a pariah; people would be standing around, laughing and chatting, and when I walked in the room, they'd stop and stare. After a while, I started to analyze every glance and comment for innuendo—it was like I was moonlighting as an anthropologist. At night, I couldn't shut up about the office to my friends. I replayed conversations to my boyfriend, acted out the way someone passed me in the hall. I knew I was being excessive, but I couldn't help myself—I was possessed by the demon spirit of my office. One night, following a particularly protracted session of role-playing, my boyfriend said, 'That's it! I can't take it! No one ever wants to get together with us because all you do is rant about your work. If you don't leave that place so we can have a normal conversation, I'm going to have you committed.' I sulked for an hour—because I knew he was right."

Oops. Sarah's nightly game of charades almost chased away the only people who *would* talk to her. Grace, a twenty-nine-year-old senior copywriter, went one step further. She didn't just jeopardize her friendships—she sacrificed them entirely.

"I'd worked hard, and was up for a promotion," Grace recalls. "After a year, new management came in—and I got nervous they wouldn't like my style. When copy came back to my desk, I scrutinized every note in the margin, every circled word, every change. I was compulsively scrupulous; I could spend twenty minutes reading a one-paragraph memo. I turned into a work machine, living in a private bubble of perfectionism; everything else ceased to exist. I stayed later and later. One night, I fell asleep at my desk and didn't realize what had happened until the security guard woke me up at three A.M. I remember sitting there, sort of bleary, and it dawned on me: This isn't normal."

No indeed. When a work obsession usurps the outside world, it's a pretty good clue something's gone awry. But while a nine-to-five fixation can skew your relationships, your personality, and valuable REM cycles, the main drain here is energy. You need a lot of gas to fuel this destructive passion. If you don't watch out, it can consume you, making you an unattractively single-track person in a multitrack world.

Such was the case for a pair of fabulously talented magazine editors we know—let's call them Sal and Helen—who worked in the same office. Shortly after meeting, the two became great friends, then writing partners. As more time passed, they formed yet another bond: an industrial-strength preoccupation with their boss, Roz. The proud owner of a mean streak the size of Texas, Roz commanded a captive and fearful audience—Sal and Helen included. Slowly but surely, their sick fascination with her grew. And grew. Until eventually, despite valiant attempts to rally, they kissed their mental health goodbye and sadly surrendered to the powerful forces of . . .

Ellen: Honestly. This is ridiculous. It's so obvious that Sal and Helen are us; we might as well just explain what happened ourselves.

Val: They are? Huh. I thought the story sounded familiar.

E: Great. Well, tell me if this rings a bell: We became full-time Roz-ometers. Our first words to each other every morning were "Have you seen Roz yet?" We scurried back and forth between our offices, reporting every movement she made. One weird twitch would require a two-hour postmortem. Then, as if a whole day of Roz-analysis wasn't enough, after work, we'd all go out for drinks, so we could spend a few more hours comparing grisly notes.

V: Oh, yeah . . . sometimes when we got home, we'd even call each other up to discuss revelations we'd had in transit.

E: Pathetic.

V: Beyond. It's all coming back to me now. Like, in the early stages, we joked about how much energy we expended on Roz, right? But after a while, we couldn't even laugh. Because it wasn't funny. It was a grand, gruesome, enveloping passion. We were victims of a sucking, whirling dervish. We writhed in the fiery bowels of hell. *We were prisoners.*

E: Okay, Val. I think you've remembered enough.

Right. At best, an office obsession merely leaves you plumb tuckered out. At worst, it can lead to self-destructive behavior; one woman we know confessed to drinking herself into oblivion every night, just so she could escape her relentless work thoughts. Not a pretty picture. In summary:

Obsession Point. What it is: The little voice in your brain that keeps reverberating "What did she mean by that, mean by that, by that, that, that?" **How it makes you feel:** Insane. Pooped. Insanely pooped. **How you should react:** Take a deep breath and try to get some distance. "Distract yourself," says Dr. Puder-York. "Read, exercise, watch television—do whatever you can to get your thoughts away from work. Challenge yourself with an activity." The further away you get, the smaller and less important everything seems. **How you do react:** You get so close, you can see the whites of your own eyes. **What you stand to lose:** Your friends. Your boyfriend. Your life. Your mind. **What you stand to gain:** Intimacy. Shared obsession with workmates can be the bonding experience of a lifetime!

2. Cape Fear

By far our most popular tourist attraction, it seems that fear and loathing in the workplace are practically the American way. What are people afraid of? You name it: bosses, shifty colleagues, the workload, the work it-self, never getting promoted, never getting a raise, never meeting that special someone (just kidding), fail-ure and rejection—and these are merely the appetizers. All of which make up one colossal main dish: unem-ploymentphobia.

The sneaky thing about fear is that, like tofu, it can manifest itself in a spooky variety of forms. In milder incarnations it can put you on the defensive, inspire you to play a blame-game of sorts in which your main motto is "But *she* said . . ." On occasion, it can cause you to lie in order to protect yourself, even if you're gener-ally a pretty honest cookie.

"Right before deadlines, my boss would go on a ram-page," says Brenda, a twenty-seven-year-old graphic artist. "I was so afraid, all I could think of was covering my ass. I delegated blame on everybody but my mother—and I would've even done that if I thought it might help. One day, I was ratting out one of the other designers, when all of a sudden, I realized I'd become a shark. My fear had turned me into a two-faced witch. It wasn't a pleasant discovery to say the least."

Don't be too hard on yourself, Brenda—desperate situations can elicit desperate measures. Ann, a thirty-year-old accountant, chose the weak, silent approach: She transformed herself into the invisible woman.

"Fear forced me underground," she says. "I was a bundle of nerves; I was petrified of getting chewed out by my boss, so I snuck around the hallways, trying to avoid her. I would leave reports in her office only when I knew she was out to lunch. I would stay until she left at night so I wouldn't have to see her in the elevator. But it wasn't just my boss. I was terrified that I'd make mistakes in my work—and the more anxious I was about making errors, the more errors I made. To avoid mishaps, I became less and less productive. Stuff piled up on my desk, and the sheer volume of the backlog scared me, too. When the phone rang, I practically jumped out of my skin. I craved Valium. I craved peace of mind."

On the other side of the spectrum, fear can surface in the form of wild, uncontrolled overachievement. When Caren, a twenty-three-year-old executive assistant, sensed her job was in jeopardy, she began a campaign to make herself Ms. Indispensable.

"I thought if I seemed eager and industrious, I could secure my spot," Caren says. "I started running into my boss's office twenty times a day to offer my services. I wrote memos with new, innovative ideas for the corporation and sent them to everyone. The problem was, I ended up annoying my boss instead of endearing myself to him. I was always in his face. I would notice he looked irritated when I interrupted him, and then I'd go back again to apologize. I couldn't help myself; my feet just kept walking in that door. To make things worse, I bit off more than I could chew—I took on so much extra work, I couldn't complete anything. I ended up looking like a disorganized busybody instead of Super-Assistant. It was a disaster."

Whether you're a rat or a mouse or merely a pest, the bottom line is, you're a scaredy-cat (and we mean that in the nicest way possible). To wit:

Cape Fear. What it is: A nightmare. **How it makes you feel:** Like you wish you could wake up, already. **How you should react:** Try to regain your footing, get a little perspective. "Identify the source of your fear," says Dr. Puder-York. "Is it your boss, your colleagues, your work? If you can define the fear, you're already depersonalizing it. This keeps the situation under control and makes you feel less like a victim." Then, ask yourself, What's the absolute worst thing that could happen here? Simple: You get fired. In the big picture, is that really so catastrophic? **How you do react:** You scream, "I'm gonna get fired! This is *catastrophic!*" **What you stand to lose:** Your grip. **What you stand to gain:** Speed—metabolism-wise, that is. You're shedding those extra, unwanted pounds like yesterday's pantyhose.

3. Self-Doubt City

This venerable metropolis is yet another common rest spot along the way . . . or is it? We're not sure. We *think* it is. Maybe. Maybe not. What do we know anyway?

You get the idea: When you're not sure about your job, everything comes into question—including yourself. A bad work situation can rattle even the most confident soul. Look at Suzanne. A thirty-two-year-old sales rep, she shot up the corporate ladder at the speed of light. Recruiters constantly wooed her; every year, her salary leapt into yet a higher tax bracket. The woman was in demand—and she knew it.

"By the time I was thirty-one, I had been promoted four times," she says. "I thought I could do no wrong—until I made a fatal move to another company. They offered me so much money, I couldn't refuse. My first day of work, I walked in, flags flying high. What I didn't realize was that my new employer's approach was totally different from what I was used to. All of a sudden, my pitches weren't right anymore. I lost a client, then another. It was the first time I'd encountered any obstacles in my career. I got nervous—and insecure. I started to second-guess everything I did. When I lost another client, I freaked out. I thought, Wait a minute. What if everything else has been a fluke—maybe this really isn't the right career for me. I should have been looking for ways to improve my selling techniques, but instead I lost all faith in myself. Luckily, I came to my senses and got back on track. But it was an unsteady time."

Suzanne was fortunate; she started out with a solid base of cocksureness. In contrast, Deena, a twenty-six-year-old bank teller, didn't have such a vast security vault to draw from—and quickly lost her balance.

"I remember the exact moment my problems started," she says. "The bank closed for the day, and we were doing our final accounting. My figures didn't add up—I was short ten dollars—and no one could leave until we straightened things out. I started to sweat. People tried to be patient, but I could tell they were annoyed. The next week, the same thing happened; two weeks later, it happened again. Technically, I wasn't at fault, but I still felt responsible. I began to dread closing time—I'd get tenser and tenser as three o'clock neared. The fourth time it happened, I turned into a nervous wreck. I imagined everyone whispering behind my back, saying what a moron I was. It didn't help that at least once a week, my boss would double-check my totals. I felt like a child, totally incapable of completing the simplest task or making a decision. The worst was when I started not being able to decide what to wear in the mornings—and then I'd be late. In the supermarket, I would agonize over which was the 'right' cereal to buy. I was only sure of one thing: That I felt inadequate and confused, every second of the day."

As we've seen, one hit of self-doubt can be potent stuff. To make matters worse, says Dr. Puder-York, "If you surrender to it, you're only putting bullets in the gun." Yeesh. In a nutshell:

Self-Doubt City. What it is: The nagging suspicion that you haven't a clue. **How it makes you feel:** Wishy-washy. Or is it washy-wishy? **How you should react:** "Don't let someone else's pathology become your own," says Dr. Puder-York. "Keep reminding yourself, 'It's not me, it's not me.' Make this your mantra." In addition, get a second opinion: Ask your friends to remind you of a time when you made a decision and it was the right one, dammit. **How you do react:** You doubt them, too. **What you stand to lose:** Self-esteem, by the boatload. **What you stand to gain:** The unique talent of seeing all sides of every issue. You could go on the road as a one-woman debate team.

4. The Lowlands

You'll find the weariest travelers in this slough of despond—their hearts are heavy, their spirits broken, and their faces, frankly, scarlet. They don't give a damn.

"After eight months of being miserable at my job, I felt flattened," says Kelly, a twenty-four-year-old paralegal. "I worked seventy-hour weeks and got yelled at by high-strung attorneys for about sixty-five of those hours. I tried so hard to please them, but they were never satisfied. After a while, everything seemed pointless. I stopped caring about anything—I'd wear the same thing to work three days in a row, I didn't put on makeup. I plodded through a dreary cycle; dragging myself to work, mechanically doing my menial tasks, dragging myself home, and then getting up the next morning and starting all over again. I felt like a hamster, spinning around and around."

Is that a blue funk in your pocket, or are you just indifferent to see us? While apathy can border on the periwinkle side of the doldrums, if you stay on the color wheel long enough, crier beware: You're bound to hit the deeper shades.

"I'd been stale at my job for six months," says Rochelle, a twenty-nine-year-old financial strategist. "I knew it was time to get out, but I couldn't muster the energy. The longer I hung around, the more exhausted I felt. It was a feat just waking up every morning. I became glum and listless—and my gloominess infected my personal life. I stopped going out. On weekends, I'd stay in bed most of the day with the shades down and the phone unplugged. I never went to the gym; I became a recluse. It was just me and my misery, wallowing together."

Basically, what we've got in these Lowlands are varying degrees of (heavy sigh) depression. No matter what the source—a broken heart, a lost puppy, a rotten job—the symptoms are easy to spot. Usually it starts with the familiar strains of lethargy, moves gradually into despair, and before you can say *Why me, why now, why?*, you're a bona fide indigo girl. You're filled with defeat and self-hate. Whereas once you were battered, now you're downright beaten. You feel like the biggest loser in the western world and beyond.

Val (tossing and turning): I know, I know, don't rub it in. I'm dead weight, a waste of space, I'll never do anything right. . . .

Ellen (shaking her): Val, wake up. Get ahold of yourself; it was only a dream.

V: (coming to with a start): Oh my god, it was so vivid,
so real. I could see Roz's face, those big, goggly eyes,
telling me how I'd screwed up again . . .

E: Shh, shh, it's okay. Everything will be all right—
uh, meanwhile, might I ask why you were napping in
the middle of a chapter?

V: Mmmmm, well, I'd call it more of a trance than a
nap. A flashback. I guess I remember those hideous
days better than I thought.

E: Do share.

V: Roz had been my boss for over a year. For a while, I
managed to keep her at bay, but in time, she started
to veer towards the psychotic. Things were coming to
a head. I felt like I was watching a huge avalanche
crashing towards me in slow motion—I was power-
less, nothing was in my control.

E: Not technically true, but . . .

V: Perception is reality. I felt completely pathetic. I
knew in my heart I was a no-talent, two-bit hack who
was trying to pass herself off as a human being. Roz
had made that clear to me.

E: Crystal.

V: Waterford. Even my outside life—what little there
was of it—seemed to disintegrate. I fought with
my boyfriend; I lost touch with any friends
who didn't work in magazines; my own precious
cat didn't want to come near me. My outside writing suffered incredibly—I had nothing left inside
me. I would skulk into work like a criminal suspect
and sit limply at my desk. Forget suspect—I was already convicted and serving what seemed like a life
sentence.

E: Every now and then, I'd try to come in and rev you up, but—

V: Nothing doing. What did it matter? I was a pawn, buffeted about by the whims of Roz. Then you blew the hatch, and two of my other friends in the office left. I had never felt so alone.

E: I hated to see you like that. The hardest thing was, although I had participated actively with you in the obsession/self-doubt/fear stages, when push came to shove, you and I went in completely opposite directions. Instead of losing hope, I lost . . .

V: Your temper? Your sense of propriety? In any case, it's true—in the final crunch, you didn't get sad, you got even. Instead of licking your wounds, you spat and bared your claws, hackles raised, ready to attack . . .

E: Wait a minute, wait a minute—hold that melodrama. Before you pounce us into the next section, let's get in a few last swipes at—

The Lowlands. What it is: Ten feet under rock bottom. **How it makes you feel:** Unworthy, paralyzed, hopeless—you've fallen and you can't get up. **How you should react:** If you can't sleep, lose your desire for food or sex, suffer constant headaches, cry spontaneously, or have recurring nightmares, put this down immediately, and find someone (professional) to talk to. If you're a paler shade of blue, though, try to rouse yourself. Indulge in an activity that you've historically enjoyed—movies, sex, shopping, eating, whatever. (Everything in moderation, of course.) Jog the fun sector of your brain. **How you do react:** You vow to cheer up, dammit. But first, a little nap. **What you stand to lose:** Thousands of dollars in therapy, if you don't extricate yourself from this rut, pronto. **What you stand**

to gain: Bedsores. And the rare opportunity to know exactly how low you can go.

5. Aggression Peak

Ellen: So, as you were saying . . .

Val: . . . Whereas I was a shrinking violet, you were no hothouse flower. In fact, you were more like a Venus flytrap—and Roz was the fly.

E: Oooooh, loving the insect analogy. Let's not exaggerate, though. Roz clearly had the upper hand—the hand that swung the ax. The fact was, as loco as she could be, the woman—and I use that term loosely—was our boss. I worked my ass off for two years, and I kissed hers almost as long. It wasn't until she suddenly turned on me . . .

V: . . . see **Chapter 8, Playing with Fire,** for details . . .

E: . . . when something inside me snapped. I couldn't pucker up anymore. I had worked too long and too hard to go through her sadistic dance. I'd paid my dues; I wasn't going to let her torture me anymore. One day, she walked into my office, bitched at me for half an hour, and then wrapped things up by saying brightly, "I don't want you to freak out about this." Of course, it was clear that she did.

V: Crystal.

E: Gayle. I felt my whole body get cold; suddenly, it dawned on me: She can't touch me. She's nothing to me. I answered . . .

V (doing her best E. imitation): "Roz, I am so *not* freaked out."

E: Precisely. She blinked a couple of times, spun on her heel, and walked out. After that, I never looked back.

When she pushed, I pushed harder. Maybe I went a little overboard with the aggression and defiance, but I wanted her to know that I wasn't going to take it anymore, that she could fire me if she wanted, that she could . . .

V: Sit on it and rotate?

E: Repeatedly.

Yes, we're a little hostile. But that's what this stage is all about: hostility. Rage. Reaching the point of no-can-do. And lest you think Ellen is an isolated case, check out Kay, a twenty-eight-year-old fury in fashion associate's clothing.

"I got to the point where I didn't care about the job at all," Kay says. "I'd already been given a warning for my bad attitude—that was the last straw—so I decided to devote all my energy to pissing people off. I'd come in late, leave early, especially when there was work to do. I'd sit at my desk, blatantly doing the crossword puzzle. Every time my boss saw me, she'd send me on yet another trip upstairs to the personnel department. My friends at work thought I was suicidal, but, to be honest, lashing out was the only way I could save my sanity. It was also pretty fun at the end—it became a sport. And I was varsity."

Sis, boom, bah. It's not as though we're condoning destructive behavior, but sometimes nice girls *do* snap. Just make sure you explode wisely. You're trying to cross a bridge, not burn it. "It's dangerous to let your emotions determine your actions in the heat of a moment," says Dr. Puder-York. "Use your anger to fuel yourself forward—talk to an attorney, explore your options. Find a way to vent productively." If you're determined to exercise the Big Bang theory, do your best to make it an educated blast. Once you've blown up a job, you can't piece it back together again. That said,

Aggression Peak. What it is: You're getting warm, warmer, hot, you're red hot—*you're on fire, you're on fire!* **How it makes you feel:** Like you've relocated to the surface of the sun. **How you should react:** Never let 'em see you sweat. Even though you're beyond the boiling point inside, outside you've got to be methodical and shrewd. When in public, keep your voice low, your guard up, and your arms down. **How you do react:** Pretty much like you should, except for the sweating. **What you stand to lose:** A job reference. **What you stand to gain:** Personal satisfaction. You get to act out at least part of your revenge fantasy—and it's magical.

Which brings us to the close of our emotional tour. Any questions? We figured as much (and good thing we were right—otherwise, the next nine chapters would've gone to waste). Truth be told, the beginning of the end is a confusing place to be. With all the obsession, fear, self-doubt, misery, and hostility muddying your brain, you're bound to be looking for some answers. Like, which is it—the beginning or the end? Is there a middle ground? How often does the average American change jobs in her lifetime? Do mosquitoes have teeth? (A little of both; not really; four to six times; no.) At this point, you're only certain of one thing: You hate your job. And while this may not seem like much, don't knock it—you have to know where you stand before you can take the first step. So, now that we've explored *how* you arrived at your hatred, let's move on to dealing with *what* you hate. Since it's always best to start big, we thought we'd kick off with the number one muse of office anxiety: Your boss. **Your Fearful Leader.**

We'll be dissecting her in **Chapter Two**—join us for the slice 'n' dice, won't you?

Break Point

Some people arrive at job misery gradually. Others experience their breaking point in a split second. "It happened all of a sudden," said every one of our Flash Gordons. "I knew I hated my job when . . ."

- I found my supervisor's stapler on my desk with a note that said, "Fill me."
- I walked into the revolving doors of my office building and "accidentally" went all the way around and walked out.
- I seriously considered moving home with my parents so I could quit.
- My left eye started to twitch when I walked into the lobby of my building.
- My cat pissed on some reports I brought home—and I didn't care.
- I ticked off the last few seconds of New Year's Eve, alone at my desk.
- I contemplated medical school—and I was an art history major.
- I got passed up for the third promotion and didn't even know until someone else in the office told me about it.
- My pubic hair went gray.
- My mother gave me career advice—and I really listened.
- I realized that I had eaten Kraft mac and cheese for a month straight because it was all I could afford.

- There was an office party and I was the only person not invited.
- My shrink suggested I come in for *two* sessions a week.
- When I asked my boss what it would take to get promoted, he said, "Lose weight."

2

Your Fearful Leader

9:36 A.M. You're en route to the office, stuck in traffic, trying to rip the stupid plastic tab off your coffee cup lid. What sadist invented these things? Whoever it was, he sucks. He sucks, work sucks, the whole concept of a capitalist society that forces you to work for a living sucks. You see yourself as one sad worker bee, buzzing around in a cold, cold cubicle. Bees suck.

You finally reach your destination and straggle into the hive. There's your lunch pal, Marnie, who nicknamed your boss Cujo. Hi, Joe from accounting—still doing research on leash laws? Hey, Stan in the corner office, how're the rabies shots holding up? The fact is, of the roughly 120 million Americans in the work force, an estimated 300 trillion* despise their bosses. You wonder at the sheer numbers. You wonder how you

*Estimate may exceed actual figure due to intensity of hatred.

managed to become one of them. You wonder how the hell capitalism ever caught on in the first place.

And it's not even 10:00 A.M.

When you get to your desk, there's a note from Dog-face herself, containing those three heart-stopping words: Please see me. Please. See. Me. Holy mother of god, *PleaseSeeMePleaseSeeMePleaseSee... shit!* Okay. Maintain calm. She probably just wants to tell you what a good job you did on the Rifkin account. Or say how much she appreciates the long hours you've been working (and hey, great outfit!). Then you wake up. *Again.* Two rude awakenings in one morning. Brutal.

As you plod miserably down the hall to her office, you decide that a meeting with your boss is like Kaddafi in a microwave: Twenty years of horror in six minutes. At the threshold of doom, you pause. Inhale, exhale. Big inhale. Your hand clenches into a fist, raises into the air, and in the milliseconds before your whitened knuckles make contact with . . . the door, you suddenly think: Why does this one woman have so much power over me? Who does she think she is?

Good questions, good questions. The answer to the first one is cyclical: She has power because she's scary; she's scary because she has power. According to Judith Sills, Ph.D., a psychologist in Philadelphia, "A boss is incredibly frightening because she can do one thing that your parents won't—take away your livelihood, put you out on the street. She doles out all the positives and negatives of your adult life: approval, support, acceptance. She can validate whether you're a good and smart person or a bad and unvalued presence. She controls the goodies of the job, and you're at her mercy."

As for who your boss thinks she is—well, that's a

little more complicated. Nonetheless, it's worth exploration. By doing research and getting to know your foe, you can be more adequately prepared to dodge his or her fire. And although no two bosses are alike, after talking to a number of boss-beaten "little people" (our tiny selves included), we've compiled résumés for the seven most common managerial types currently stalking the workplace. What's your poison? Read on.

Mr. Right-And-Don't-You-Forget-It

Career Objective: To transform you into the ultimate Yes-Woman

Work Experience: Brooks no dissent. Insists that his approach—however harebrained—is the only approach; subsequently, assumes your methods are inherently flawed. Does things his way.

Special Skills: Bulldozing

Education: John Deerefield Academy

References: Frank Sinatra

To quote one of this species, "The office is not a democracy." As king, your boss considers his judgment to be the law of the land. Which pretty much throws any input you might have directly into the moat. Worst of all, when you timidly suggest the earth *might not actually be flat*, he banishes you to your office to draw a map of the world. His world. Degrading? Yep. But as the crayons break in your hand out of frustration, you know that you only have two choices: Concur or be conquered.

"With my boss, it was her way or the highway," says Pamela, a twenty-seven-year-old television producer. "She had no faith in us—she insisted on seeing every single thing we generated; she accompanied us to meetings. She even went through our desks and 'accidentally' opened our mail. It was her way of keeping tabs on us, pointing out the various ways we'd screwed up without her tutelage. She made it clear that anything we could do, she could do better. No one dared complain, though. It was a small office, and she would've made life very unpleasant if we had."

While Pamela opted to take the concession stand, Mandy, a twenty-nine-year-old events planner, tried to fight the tide—and nearly drowned.

"I was in a meeting with the top people in our department," recounts Mandy. "We were trying to come up with a theme for a corporate shindig. My boss came up with what she thought was a brilliant idea:—black and white party decorations. Stupid, stupid, stupid: The company in question was currently under fire for racial discrimination—what could be worse? When I mentioned this conflict, she ignored me and kept talking, but when other people agreed with me, she tried to cover by saying, 'Of course I knew that. I was trying to imply racial harmony. It would be an ebony and ivory kind of thing.' Please. We finally decided on a nautical theme, but the damage was done. Right after that, she practically blackballed me from the department. She told everyone I wasn't a team player, that I was only interested in making trouble. Thank god I got transferred to another department."

When it comes to Mr. Right-And-Don't-You-Forget-It, if you want to play his game, you've got to abide by his rules. Fortunately, there's only one rule, and it's very simple. Unfortunately, that rule reads: Do as I say, not as you say. Of course, if you want to play it safe, you can just go along with him. "Most of us know of colleagues who spoke their minds and got punished for it," says Ellen Bravo, the director of 9 to 5, an organization for women in the workplace. "On the other hand, if your boss is a reasonable human being, you can try appealing to him with humor or logic. If the conflict is based on subjective opinion, defer to him. But if it's fact-based, ask for a chance to do some research and find the real answer. Say, 'If I'm wrong, I'm happy to admit it; if I'm right, we'll both benefit.' Don't be antagonistic, but take the initiative—and then if you can, clearly prove your point." Moreover, don't treat your boss like an opponent; let him know you're a member of his team.

Giant caveat: If your manager veers toward the despotic, all the logic in the world won't set him straight. In this case, you'll just have to accept the fact that you can't teach an old (deluded, flea-bitten) cur new tricks. He's never going to roll over. So keep your mouth shut—with just enough space left open to bite the bullet. Every dog has his day.

SVENGALI

Career Objective: To make his perception your reality

Work Experience: Acts as casting director. Chooses your part in the office power play—be it leading role or understudy. Assigns and reassigns roles at will. Induces chronic schizophrenia.

Special Skills: Pigeonholing

Education: Defining U.

References: Noah Webster

It's the big question of the morning as you sit down with your coffee and paper: Who will I be today? The dullard? The slacker? Or maybe even . . . the star? Of course, it's not really up to you—your boss is calling the shots. And if you think your appointed role has anything to do with your job performance, the only part you'll ever play is the naïf.

Some defining bosses like to cast their employees in stone from the get-go. "I had been working for a month, and things were going fine," says Terry, a twenty-five-year-old magazine researcher. "Then one Friday, I had to leave the office early to catch a plane; in the rush, a mistake got into an article. When I got back to the office on Monday, my boss called me in and informed me of the error. I apologized profusely, but after that, I noticed a shift in the climate. It was as if I suddenly had the word 'slipshod' branded on my forehead. He had other people read over my work, gave me boring, busy-work assignments, and basically never trusted me again. One tiny slip-up affected my entire future in that office."

For some managers, first impressions are damning. The cement settles around your persona, and before you can say "Mann's Chinese Theatre" you're totally non grata. But there's also a breed of pigeonholers that's somewhat more mercurial. And frankly, the frequent costume changes can put an ugly wrinkle in your workday.

"My first eight months on the job, my boss was convinced I was brilliant. He called me his model student," says Julie, a political strategist. "Then I started dating someone from a rival political camp. My boss got paranoid that I was secretly planning to sabotage him, and suddenly, he decided my work was no good. He told a coworker that I was Mata Hari, without the looks. After a few more months, the relationship ended for personal reasons. With this breakup, I was magically redeemed.

My boss assumed the split was over political differences—and he liked that. I became his office pet again. That's when I realized his perception of me as a person mattered far more than my actual work."

Life with Svengali can lead to an identity crisis. You don't know who you are—and neither do you. Consequently, when your boss is categorizing you for the hundredth time (that day), your first inclination might be to protest, "But *yesterday* you said!" Before you pipe up, however, do some background work on your current character. For example, have you been typecast as a slacker because you come in late? Or because you conduct personal phone conversations a mite too audibly? If your dramatis persona bears even the slightest resemblance to your true identity, says Dr. Sills, then your best bet is to "go in vivid opposition to the stereotype. Make a big production of coming in at eight-thirty A.M., or staying through dinner. Showboat your hard work, your energy, your efforts to change."

If, on the other hand, you've done some honest soul-searching and truly believe you've been miscast, you'll have to stick with the program or go on the road. To keep your perspective, view this as a temporary fictional role. You can always save the real you for the outside world (you know, that place you crawl through every night on your way home so that you can get some sleep so that you can be in to work early the next morning). In the meantime, the play's the thing.

SYBIL

Career Objective: Changes all the time
Work Experience: Deftly drives emotional jags; shifts gears at ninety miles an hour. Does lightning-fast al-

terations on her moods—and thus, yours. Never fails to surprise and confuse.

Special Skills: Morphing
Education: Barbizon School of (Re)Modeling (Be a multiple personality—or just look like one!)
References: Michael Jackson

Every day's a surprise party in this office. Unlike Svengali, who shuffles your identities faster than a blackjack dealer, Sybil plays every face card herself. She—or should we say *they*—treats you to a front-row seat of personalities on parade. Furthermore, she can go from sunny, to partly cloudy, to mostly cloudy, to kind of rainy, to really stormy, to totally hurricaney, back to partly sunny before you can even finish reading this sentence. As a result, you're in a constant state of flux, trying to figure out (a) what the current climate is and (b) how you should dress for it.

Easier said than done. Predictions about this type of boss are never watertight—the best you can do is keep an eye out for indicators. Sometimes, the warning signals are physically manifested. "My boss's breakfast clued us into her moods," recalls Jenny, a twenty-three-year-old fashion retailer. "She once told us she ate fattening foods when she was depressed, and after that, we watched her morning intake like hawks. If she had fruit and black coffee, we knew she was feeling in control and would be efficient, no-nonsense. Cheese Danish or doughnuts presaged snappish and irrational behavior. Cereal and yogurt meant a happier medium. We prayed for those Grape Nuts days." In the case of LeeAnn, a twenty-eight-year-old cosmetics marketer, emergency lights flashed when her boss wore a certain brooch on her lapel. "The pin was engraved with her family coat-of-arms," LeeAnn says. "She said it signified readiness to do battle. And sure enough, every time she slapped that sucker on her suit jacket, we knew she was on the warpath—and we'd steer clear."

Other times, the cues are more subtle. For Maggie, a twenty-nine-year-old business administrator, her supervisor's phone manner was the tip-off. "When he answered with his name, he was liking himself and feeling confident. When he answered with the company name, he was feeling harried and pressured. When he said a plain 'hello,' he would be particularly jokey and intimate with us. Worst was when he wouldn't answer at all. Those days, he'd be especially antagonistic—and we'd keep our distance until he picked up the phone again."

So take time to study the meteorological signs. If you can tell which way the wind is blowing, you'll decrease your chances of losing your shirt. Then again, your measurements may be skewed by the sheer velocity of the mood changes. Working for Sybil can be like playing hopscotch on a minefield: One second it's fun and games, the next second it's guns and flames.

"Our manager could go from zero to sixty, back to zero in two minutes flat," recounts Yvette, a twenty-seven-year-old book editor. "She was the ultimate roller coaster. She'd be all happy in the morning and invite us out to lunch. Then, if something set her off before noon—a fight with her boyfriend, a rip in her stockings, anything—when we showed up at her door, she'd snap, 'If you were as interested in your work as you are in food, maybe we'd see some progress around here!' It was nerve-racking because we never knew what was coming."

Wait, there's more: With so many visages at her disposal, Sybil doesn't always feel compelled to only wear one at a time. Result: The woman can be as phony and two-faced as a wooden nickel. "You never really knew where you stood with our department head," says Jo, a thirty-year-old money manager, "because he'd never say anything up-front—he'd simply bad-mouth you to everyone else. He was sweet as pie to your face, but then you'd hear that he spent the afternoon shitting all over you to other people in the department. It made us all paranoid."

When you're a Sybil-servant, the effects are circular: Her moodiness makes you confused; your confusion makes you edgy; the edginess makes you exhausted; the exhaustion makes *you* moody. And before you know it, *you're* the one making conference calls to you, yourself, and you. Stop. Rewind. Push *Play.* As Dr. Sills says, "You are not the center of her universe—although she may be the center of yours—and you are not responsible for her behavior. So identify her mood, and then realize that you didn't cause it, that she actually has a life apart from you." What's more, if you sense she's playing foul, stay off her field and lay low—long distance is the next best thing to being outta there. If physical distance isn't feasible, do your best to maintain emotional space. You don't have to catch the wave if you don't want to.

THE ROBBER BARON

Career Objective: To reap, consume, digest, and pass the fruits of your labor

Work Experience: Performs extensive credit checks. Appropriates what's yours as his—unless it's bad, in which case it's resoundingly yours.
Special Skills: Sponging
Education: Using U.
References: Tom Arnold

You've come up with a stellar idea for Project X. God, you're good. At the department meeting later that afternoon, you notice that all the way-higher-ups are patting your boss on the back and saying, "Great work on that Project X." Odd. Three days later, the X corporation has nixed your company's pitch. And now, everyone from the way-higher-ups to the way-low-downs suddenly knows that this was all your terrible idea. What happened?

Duh. Taking credit and passing blame are this boss's greatest pastimes. Witness Laura, a twenty-three-year-old magazine editorial assistant, who worked for a wolf in Chanel clothing—and got fleeced by her devious designs.

"We had each been asked to submit six story ideas by the end of the day," says Laura. "That morning, I was working on them at my computer, and the editor I assisted—a notorious idea-klepto—read them over my shoulder. Two minutes later, she handed me a pile of letters and asked me to type them, right away—before I did anything else. She went back into her office and shut the door. In about half an hour, she came rushing out, and snatched up a printout as it was coming out of the department printer. When I asked her what it was, she said, 'Nothing, only my article ideas—I'd show them to you, but I'm too embarrassed. I'm just going to hand them in and forget about them.' I smelled a rat. At lunch, she went to her gym, and while a friend guarded the door, I went into her computer files. My heart was pounding, but I had to see what her ideas were. Sure enough, she completely ripped me off—she plagiarized five out of my six story topics. Meanwhile, she had stalled me by giving me those letters to type so she could hand her memo in first. I was screwed—if I submitted mine, it would look like I'd copied her."

Laura's boss chose the sly, sneaky approach. Other robber barons opt to rape and pillage in broad daylight.

"My boss always said it was my job to make him look good," says Jean, a twenty-nine-year-old stock market analyst. "One day, a television show wanted to interview him as a money expert. He was terrified—he wasn't the most articulate guy—and asked me to go to the taping with him. It turned out that as soon as the cameras started rolling, he became a blithering idiot. So he devised this system: The interviewer asked the question, and then they'd stop filming while I frantically thought of an answer, typed it up, and handed it to my boss. He would read it, and they'd start taping again while he rattled off whatever I had written. Basically, I was feeding him words, running back and forth like a trained chimp. He treated me like a slave—at the end of the whole, arduous process, he never even thanked me. When the show finally ran, everyone in the office was telling him how great he was on television. He said, 'What can I say, I guess I'm a natural.' "

Yeah, a natural *thief.* As an employee of The Robber Baron, you may find yourself doing two jobs for the low, low price of one. He's a sharing sort of fellow, who generally embraces the motto *Mí trabajo, su trabajo.* Translation: You carry the lazy swine like a rickshaw. What you want to do is storm into his office and say something really pithy like "That was mine, mine, all mine!" Don't. An alternative approach, says Ellen Bravo, is to send him a memo saying, 'I'm so happy that you liked my report, but I was disappointed you didn't mention it was my idea and my work. I'd really appreciate it if you'd let people know.' If he ignores you, pass the memo on to his boss or to other employees." Okely-dokely. In a pink-sky world this is a swell-sounding tactic, but you could end up hosing yourself. So proceed with caution. Ask yourself: What are the costs versus the benefits? While you can't win by doing nothing, be aware that taking action can incur *either* a loss or a gain. Then again, "Are you striving to advance his career or yours?" asks Bravo. Something worth mulling over. In the meantime, protect yourself. Don't discuss an idea until you've put it in writing. Keep notes and write memos like a maniac. If none of this works, maybe it's time to take those clever ideas elsewhere.

Vampira

Career Objective: To suck the lifeblood out of you

Work Experience: Holds you hostage—chains you to your desk on weekends and late nights. Accounts for twenty-seven hours of your day, every day. Devours your social life.

Special Skills: Liposuction

Education: Transylvania College (night school)

References: Available upon inquest

It's Friday evening, and you have theater tickets. The show starts in half an hour—there's just enough time to get there, if you hop a cab. Except. Your boss ordered you not to budge until she gives exit permission. You keep peeking into her office to see if her light's on. It is, natch. The woman never has any weekend plans, so she often stays for all eternity, which means you have to stay all eternity plus ten minutes. Meanwhile, you swear you can hear her in there having phone sex with her overseas boyfriend. Great—she's giggling like anybody's nickel whore, and you paid eighty bucks *not* to watch a bunch of people in rags sing about the French Revolution.

On the other hand, why see *Les Misérables* when you live it? Here in Office Entebbe, there's no escape. "I was putting in fourteen-hour days," says Glenda, a twenty-five-year-old product coordinator at a record company. "My boss was a workaholic, and she expected everyone to share her addiction. Work was her whole life; she refused to accept that anyone would have any social obligations or responsibilities. When new hires came—turnover was high—we'd ask them if they had a boyfriend or girlfriend. If they said yes, we'd say, 'Take a picture so you remember what they look like.' Competing companies even joked that our label had the highest divorce rate. Our boss watched us like a prison warden. One day at noon, I went to visit a friend in the hospital and brought back a sandwich to eat at my desk. My boss saw me unwrapping it and said, 'You've been gone for an hour—if you leave the office at lunchtime, you have to eat outside the office.' And then she forced me to throw my sandwich in the garbage. I was starving, but I didn't dare fish it out."

Talk about bad diets. Frequently, hostage taking even exceeds office territory. Just when you thought it was safe to go into your living room . . .

"My supervisor used to call me at home—late at night, on weekends, even during holidays," says Janet, a twenty-four-year-old arbitrage assistant. "I was her shrink, her slave, her chief nursemaid and bottle washer; she expected me to be on call for both business and social functions. One Labor Day weekend, I had to go to California to be a bridesmaid in a wedding. At the last minute, she made me change my plane reservation so I could work an extra day. I missed the rehearsal dinner, but I felt like I was lucky to get away at all, so I didn't complain. Before I took off, I made the mistake of telling my boss the name of the hotel where I was staying. That night, I got an urgent message from the switchboard telling me to call her, no matter what hour. I phoned back—it was past midnight, her time—and she informed me there was a crisis. She had rebooked me on an earlier flight returning first thing the next morning. When I got to the office, all jet-lagged from flying cross country and back in twenty-four hours, the 'crisis' turned out to be that she and her boyfriend had had a huge fight. I was furious with her—and almost more furious with myself for actually obeying her orders."

Working for Vampira can leave you feeling drained. You'd like to do your best Moses impression, entreating her to "Let my person go," but you're too afraid of her deadly bite to do much more than sit like a toady— quivering ... subservient ... employed. Ellen Bravo suggests you ask her to "Name her office policy. Get her to articulate your working hours—in writing, if possible. Establish an agreement and then make sure that both you and she stick to it. Of course, if there's a crisis, you have to be flexible, but otherwise, a formal policy will limit arbitrary behavior." Again, keep yourself covered: Get all your work done, arrange for someone to fill in for you if you go on vacation, make sure you're reproof-proof. As for socializing with the Princess of Darkness, be polite, but firm—make pleasant, innocuous excuses that are airtight. Be a nerd by day—someone she'd want to work with but not play with. Quick tip for the future? Before you take your next job, poke around and find out if giving blood is a prerequisite.

MOLOTOV

Career Objective: To explode in your face
Work Experience: Erupts at a moment's notice. Rants and raves loudly and freely. Excels at ax-wielding and boom-dropping.
Special Skills: Bang! Pow! Whammo!
Education: NASA
References: Guy Fawkes

This boss is a dynamo—literally. He's a true Type A (as in Atomic) and rules with an iron lung. Needless to say, his tantrums are ballistic and unpredictable. What's weird is that this boss can also be charming and conciliatory. He may spew lava, but after Pompeii cools—and you've turned into a statue—he's apt to stick his head in your office and make small talk. You want to believe that it won't happen again, and so you stick around—only to get blown sky-high another time. And the cycle, as is its wont, keeps coming to a boil.

"My boss had a terrible temper," says Moira, a twenty-nine-year-old catalogue designer. "He was completely incapable of controlling his anger. One morning, my phone rang. When I picked it up, all I heard was his shaky, enraged whisper. *'Get in here.'* I went down the hall to his office—the longest twenty steps of my life—and walked in his door. The photo editor was sitting on his couch. When I saw her face, I knew she had informed on me. I didn't blame her—he probably shook her down. Evidently, I hadn't given her some photo credits she needed. My boss's face was white. If there had been newspaper in his office, it would have burst into flame. He stuck his finger so close to my face, I could have bitten it off, had I dared open my mouth. For about twenty minutes, he screamed at the photo editor about all my obvious flaws. When he got tired of that, he unleashed on me. I was terrified. He yelled at me so badly, I felt like a circus freak."

Is it over? Can we look now? Viewer discretion is advised: This kind of boss can get even scarier. The ugly truth is, some flamethrowers don't confine themselves to mere verbal fire, they actually get physical. The horror studies abound:

- "I walked into my managing director's office to tell him I couldn't make the afternoon meeting. He was eating breakfast, and the next thing I knew, he was whipping his muffin at me and screaming 'Fuck you!' I ran out in a flurry of bran."
- "I was standing in the doorway of my boss's office and we were arguing. He jumped up, slammed the door shut in my face—literally—and broke my nose. He wouldn't even pay my health insurance deductible."
- "My supervisor needed some videotapes for a presentation. He kept shrieking, 'Where are the tapes? Where are the tapes?' I tried to tell him, but he wouldn't listen. He got so worked up, he picked up a stack of videos from his desk—the ones he was look-

ing for, incidentally—and hurled them at my head. I ducked, and he hit a framed print. The glass shattered everywhere."

- "My boss was famous for her violent nature. One day, I was late on a project; she got so infuriated, she started pounding her fists on her desk, swept all the papers off of it with her arm, and then pushed her chair back with such fury, she tipped over backwards. I would've laughed my ass off if I hadn't been so terrified."

- "We were standing in the hallway, and I apologetically told my boss that I had lost a client. She looked at me with total disgust, spat on my shoes, then turned and walked away."

Basically, we're talking battered-employee syndrome here—and you're the statistic. Molotov types can wreak havoc on the nerves, so if you can't figure out a way to defect, you'll probably end up walking softly and carrying a big grudge. While you're there, do your best to deflect the shrapnel. "To a certain extent, listening to your boss vent is a part of every job," says Dr. Sills. "But you don't have to internalize it. Look as though you're paying attention, but during the course of his rant, sing 'The Star-Spangled Banner' in your head. Never tolerate verbal abuse. Say, 'I'm not comfortable being called names; it would be more constructive to discuss this when you're calmer,' and then walk away. And don't get defensive; it'll only trap you. If you simply agree with him, you'll get out of the office—and his line of fire—more quickly."

THE WAFFLER

Career Objective: At this point, we don't know

Work Experience: Firmly believes in something—until he doesn't. Procrastinates because he just can't make up his mind. Forces you to make a decision for him—and then punishes you for it. Denies everything.

Special Skills: Shilly-shallying

Education: Harvard. No, Yale. No, Harvard.

References: Bill Clinton

If Molotov is the IRA, the Waffler is the IRS—slow, inefficient, hard to decipher. Call him the Crisco Kid; he can't stick to anything. Indecision is his modus operandi; his convictions have the life span and focus of a fruit fly. To coin the old song: He says potato, he says potahto; he says tomato, he says tomahto—quick instrumental—let's call the whole thing off.

Unlike some of his more antagonistic counterparts, this species usually has a warm heart. Unfortunately, he also has cold feet—which are continually moving one step up and two steps back—and herein lies the rub. "I was working on a big bankruptcy case," says Hannah, a twenty-nine-year-old corporate lawyer. "We ended up working until two A.M. every day because my boss couldn't commit to a decision. He'd make us repeat work, re-research things—basically do useless tasks—so he could have more time to think things over. You'd hustle your ass off to get something done by Monday, and then it would sit on his desk until Friday because he wouldn't know what to do with it. We rushed to file documents with the court, just under the wire, because he was such a staller. Worse, he would always litigate instead of settling a case because he couldn't make up his mind so early on. He was never angry or hostile; he was governed more by stupidity than malice. Nonetheless, we had to be at his beck and call around the clock, on the off chance that he might actually make a move."

In addition to moving at the speed of the continental drift, The Waffler is also infuriatingly vague. "Our bureau chief could never come up with solid guidelines," says Mindy, a twenty-eight-year-old newswriter. "He'd say things like, 'I want this story to be smart and good.' Oh, I would think, I guess we got our wires crossed, I thought you wanted this to be dumb and bad. When I pressed him for more concrete comments, he would either hem and haw or suggest we talk about it later, tomorrow, in an hour. He was congenitally incapable of specificity. And when he didn't like something—which was often—he would send you back to fix it. The problem was, you had no clear idea what needed to be fixed. He only knew what was wrong—and it was our job to fumble around trying to figure out what could possibly be right. It was like working on a game show, where no one had the answers."

Talk about double jeopardy. Or make that a triple. The thing about this boss is that his paralysis and revisionist tendencies usually stem from his own fears and insecurities. In fact, many employees we spoke to told us they felt responsible for, even protective of, their tormented supervisors. "He depended on me," said one woman. "He seemed so pathetic and helpless all the time. He *needed* me." Don't fool yourself. Says Dr. Sills, "There's a thin line between compassion and contempt. And contempt for your boss translates to contempt for your job." So skip the savior act and start thinking about the cross you have to bear. Pity is *not* good enough reason to suffer the exasperating, time-burning techniques

The Waffler favors. Give your blood pressure a break: Leggo this Eggo.

Which brings us to the most heinous boss duo of all: The Sexual Harasser and The Discriminator. No joke résumés, no funny nicknames—working for these two types of bosses is no laughing matter. Because it's too serious a subject to be glib about (although we do so love to be glib), we're going to keep this short and to the point. Michael Widomski, a public affairs special- ist at the Equal Employment Opportunity Commis- sion (EEOC), defines sexual harassment as any verbal or physical behavior of a sexual nature that's un- wanted, offensive, and repeated and which interferes with your ability to keep or do your job. Such harass- ment is illegal if "going along" becomes a condition of your employment, is necessary for setting terms of employment, or if the purpose of the harassment is such that it interferes with work performance and/or creates a hostile environment. Got it? When you re- ceive unequal treatment from an employer (or during the employment process) as a result of race, religion, sex, national origin, age, or disability—*that's* discrimi- nation.

If these situations apply to you, try these numbers on for size:

- 9 to 5, The National Association for Working Women. For advice and information, call (800) 522-0925.
- EEOC. For written information, call (800) 669-3362; for advice on your legal rights, call (800) 669-4000.

One last bit of editorializing (because we do so love to editorialize): Harassment and discrimination are *not your fault.* How you respond to them is your choice. You're under no obligation to be a hero, or a martyr, or a role model. Although actions certainly speak louder than quiet suffering, your primary obligation is to pick the route that's emotionally most effective and comfortable for you. And whatever that route might be, we're right there behind you. Case closed.

3

Work/Counterwork

10:15 A.M. You've been standing outside your boss's office for ten minutes now. If it was so urgent, why is she making you wait? You're fixing your bangs for the thirty-seventh time when her door swings open. Cue to enter. You try to make happy-face and swagger in like a matador, but you're afraid you look more like a wounded bull. Your boss nods toward a chair: Cue to sit. Pause, pause, pause—and the picador strikes. "This lateness is unacceptable," she hisses. "You *will* be in at nine A.M. on the dot. To ensure this, I'd like you to turn on my coffee machine, first thing every morning, so I know you're here and ready to work. You're on thin ice, so you'd better not screw up again. Got it?" This would be your cue to speak. As your panicked consciousness struggles to construct an apology, Satan mounts your larynx. "Yeah, I got it," you hear a voice that sounds remarkably like yours saying somewhere in the room.

"But the way I see it, I work until ten o'clock almost every night. So even if I'm in a little late, you're getting your money's worth out of me. Also, I don't recall coffee making being part of my job description. I'll do my best to be punctual, but I'm not here to be degraded."

Dead silence. Neither of you can believe what you just heard. Especially you. Your boss's face looks like it's about to hatch. "Is that so?" she asks. "The way I see it, other people in this office stay until midnight and still come in on time. We're working our butts off, so don't you swagger in like a happy-faced matador and give me attitude. This is my office, and while you're in it, you'll abide by my rules. Now why don't you go back to your desk and stop wasting my time?"

Definite cue to leave. You quiver back down the hall and see Stan and Marnie looking at you anxiously. You'll fill them in later—right now, you need to be alone. As you weakly sit at your desk, one hot tear burns a slow trail down your nose. Well, the good news is, you actually pulled off the happy matador bit. The bad news is, you still got trampled. And while you're sitting here—swollen, dejected, your whole day shattered—she's probably clam-happy, plotting the next phase of your demise.

Or is she? What you don't know about your boss might surprise you. Don't get us wrong: We're not trying to defend her or anything. However, it's important to acknowledge that there are two sides to every tale of woe. As such, we've decided to give the bosses of the world some airtime (not that we care about their stinking opinions but fair's fair). To square the scales, for each boss's scenario, we'll provide the corresponding employee's version of the same scenario. With luck, getting the view from both sides of the ladder will make your climb less clumsy. Plus, a little voyeurism is always a treat. So below, four real-life horror stories, eight great versions. Yes, folks, it's time to play (Maestro, some game show theme music, please) . . .

Whose Fault Is It Anyway?! *The exciting game show where bosses and employees match tales of truth and consequence, hope and horror, ball-busting and bad-mouthing, in an attempt to win the ultimate prize of Being Right. Entering the studio now are our first two contestants. Jane is a twenty-four-year-old editorial assistant from Chicago; her opponent—and ex-boss—Rachel, is a thirty-two-year-old editor at a top consumer magazine. While Rachel steps into our special soundproof booth, Jane will have ninety seconds to state her case. Are you ready, Jane? Go!*

Jane: I'd been working a year when Rachel became my boss. The first task she gave me: cleaning out her new office. When I told her I had to finish an urgent project for another editor first, she blew her stack. It was a rattling way to start. From that point on, everything I did fell short. Once she asked me for manila folders, and when I gave her envelopes by mistake, she screamed accusations that I was trying to make her job harder. I mean, Jesus! Out of desperation, I went to talk to our personnel manager. She just patted my hand and told me it wasn't a big deal. No big deal? I was drowning in my own nervous sweat.

Next, my desk was moved to right outside Rachel's office—every morning, she'd stomp past me without even saying hello. Now that I was so close, she had a whole new battery of gripes: My personal calls, my attitude, my hours. I was in a constant state of anxiety. I did whatever I could to keep contact to a minimum. And while I tried to limit my personal calls, talking to my friends was the only thing that kept me sane.

I often worked late nights because I was trying to take on more responsibilities in hopes of moving up. One Monday, Rachel called me into her office. Evidently, I had filed for something like twenty hours overtime in one week—and Rachel was livid. She asked if I was trying to scam the company out of money. I was speechless; and she interpreted my silence as an admission of guilt. She then decreed that I had to leave the building at six P.M. every day. If my work wasn't done by then, I had to take it home with me.

Nothing pleased her. One time, she asked me to type a long manuscript and I said, "Sure, I like inputting." Rachel smirked and said, "That goody-two-shoes attitude doesn't work with me." I mean, can you believe it? She hated me—that was clear. What had I done? The whole scene was monstrous; by the time I got fired, I was relieved.

Thank you, Jane. And now, let's bring Rachel back into the studio. All set? The clock . . . starts . . . now!

Rachel: The day Jane became my assistant, I was moving into another office that was filled with boxes of junk. I had to get it cleared out in an hour if I wanted bookshelves installed, so I called Jane and asked her to help me. She said she was too busy. The nerve! Maybe I lost my temper, but it was her fault. From that moment on, I knew I'd never like her.

I always meant to take her out to lunch to bond, but I couldn't bear the thought of spending a whole hour with her. She was such a snippy little thing. She'd come into my office, drop stuff on my desk, say "Here," and then prance out like she was doing me some giant favor. When she screwed up—which was often—she never explained or apologized. I'd tell her what she did wrong in an effort to teach her, and she'd just wince and skulk out. I may have seemed impatient, but it was one bungle after another. For example, one time she brought me some envelopes, plopped them on my desk, and said "Envelopes" in this amazingly snotty tone. I'd asked for folders, actually, but that wasn't what bothered me. It was her rudeness. Was I not allowed to ask her to get me office supplies? I gave her a talk about her attitude problem, but she just sat there, sullen. She didn't care.

The last straw was when I got a call from my boss saying that Jane had put in for forty hours of overtime in one week. She was obviously trying to soak the company for all the money she could. I hated what a scammer she was. She expensed everything: taxis, messengers, lunches, what have you. How can something be a work expense when you're not doing any work?

Okay, Rachel, time's up. Now that we've heard both sides of this saga, let's turn to our judges for a verdict.

Meaning us, of course. Okay, **what happened here?** A classic instance of hate at first sight. Jane and Rachel started off on the wrong foot, and their relationship just got lamer and lamer. **Then what?** Jane became Jell-O-Woman, while Rachel went flambé. No just desserts here: Rachel's brusque demands spurred Jane's fear; Jane's fear led to work mistakes; the work mistakes sparked Rachel's anger; and the dog kept chasing its tail. **Could they have turned it around?** Mmm ... maybe. However, this would have required Rachel to do some serious behavior modification, and chill out, such that Jane could stop doing her dance of (scared to) death. In other words, they'd need complete personality makeovers—be different people, living in a different time, on a different planet. So, no. They didn't stand a chance. Then, **Whose fault is it anyway?** To be honest, Ellen had a dram of empathy for Rachel's frustration (she herself once had had a nonproductive assistant). But, Val (Ellen's allegedly "nonproductive" assistant) loudly and stridently condemned Rachel for her excessive harshness. Due to Val's impassioned—not to mention high-decibel—arguments, the burden of blame ultimately landed on Rachel's chip-littered shoulders. **Why?** Because a good boss, no matter how exasperated, should be able to refrain from crossing the line of professionalism into terrorism. Finally, **Where are they now?** Rachel is presently trying to hire another assistant and, in the interim, gets her own office supplies. Jane is rebuilding her confidence in graduate school.

Which brings us to round two. Our second pair of contestants: Vanessa, a twenty-four-year-old curatorial assistant in a New York museum, and Harry, forty-two, her direct supervisor and a head curator. Harry, you'll be escorted to our soundproof booth; Vanessa, you're up. Ready—begin!

Vanessa: When I started working at the museum, my boss, Harry, was very nice to me. The first year, I was extremely eager to please. But the administrative tasks soon grew boring; I itched to do something more creative. I mean, I'd graduated with honors, and had been accepted to major art-restoration programs across the country—typing and answering the phone weren't exactly my calling. Finally, I got the chance to curate small exhibits: office atriums, shopping plazas, that sort of thing. I loved it—every time there was a smallish show, I would volunteer to oversee it.

The more "good" stuff I got to do, the more I neglected my administrative duties. My desk overflowed with unfinished paperwork, but Harry hired an office temp, so I figured I was covered. Since everyone kept telling me how great my curating was, I didn't worry about the other stuff. So when Harry told me my yearly raise was being withheld due to poor performance, I was floored. He said he had faith I would pick up my slack, and in four months we'd talk again. I was pissed, but I sucked it up and pretended to be the perkiest cotton-picking Xerox girl in the world.

Then another assistant—one who started six months after me—got promoted to assistant curator. I asked Harry why I was passed over, and he said I had to excel in my current job before I could move up. How are you supposed to "excel" in grunt work? At any rate, I went along with their silly game, and after four months I got the raise. A month later, another curator slot opened up—this time they hired someone from the outside. What was wrong with these people? Hadn't I paid enough dues already? I bitched to anyone who would listen. I wanted them to be scared to lose me. I probably should've looked for another job, but I liked hanging out with my office friends. I even liked Harry; I just wished he'd wise up and see what a gold mine I was.

New Year's came and went. I took matters into my

own hands and asked Harry's boss—the museum director—for a title change. He said he'd discuss it with Harry. The next thing I knew, Harry summoned me into the conference room for a talk. I thought he was going to tell me I'd been promoted. Instead, he asked if I had any idea what a breach of protocol it was for me to go over his head. Well, no, I didn't. He then said that he had to let me go. I was shocked. He added that everyone really liked me, but my work wasn't up to snuff. Harry seemed to feel bad about it—but I felt worse. In my heart, I knew that it was for the best, but I would have liked to make the decision myself.

Artfully done, Vanessa. Now, let's see how Harry paints the picture. Ninety seconds on the clock . . . okay, you're on.

Harry: I trained Vanessa. She was extremely bright, learned fast, and we got along well. The first year went smoothly. In the second year, she started to do some small curatorial assignments—and then the attitude problem began. She was young and arrogant; she thought administrative tasks were beneath her. She was so delinquent, we actually had to hire office temps—at which point, she started delegating her work to them so she could devote herself to more fun projects.

By the time she was due for a raise, her performance had deteriorated drastically. We also had complaints from artists: She was rude to them; they didn't want to work with her. So instead of giving her a merit increase, we put her on probation and let her know what the problems were, hoping she'd straighten out. She seemed to understand. Although she was obviously angry, her work improved and we gave her a salary increase, but not a promotion. This frustrated her; she started doing blatantly hostile things, like sitting at her desk and openly reading a book. Politically, she didn't know when to keep her mouth shut. She was unhappy and wanted us to know it. One day, she marched upstairs to the museum director's office and said, "I want a promotion." Of course, it's good to take initiative, but the way she expressed herself was off-putting. She expected rewards, but didn't seem to realize that she had to shape up in order to get them.

Despite everything, we all felt very fond of her and were more lax than we should have been. Nevertheless, her work was too unreliable. I agonized over the situation. I liked her so much; why wouldn't she just apply herself? I couldn't sleep. Had I been more experienced, I might not have let things drag on for so long. Finally, I knew I had to dismiss her. And although I felt extremely sad, as soon as I made the decision I was relieved.

We appreciate your candor, Harry. Now, it's time to consult our judges.

Hi. Us again. **What happened here?** In our opinion, this was a textbook case of assistant-itis: Basically, Vanessa got so sick of entry-level drudgery, she created some serious ill will. **Then what?** The situation became chronic. Her virulent attitude and chronic malaise eroded her work habits and created disorder. Unfortunately, she was blind to her condition, immune to criticism and advice. Although Harry tried to rehabilitate her in an attempt to ward off radical surgery, she resisted medication. Thus, in the end, she had a bitter pill to swallow. **Could they have turned it around?** Well, let's consult her chart. Considering the severity of her symptoms, achieving remission would have required treatment, to wipe out the, uh, *contagion* that caused her to manifest feelings of . . . (Dammit, Jim, we're writers, not doctors!). She was too pig-stubborn to budge, okay? Well then, **Whose fault is it anyway?** Unanimous vote: Vanessa wins the blame game, hands down. **Why?** Because she acted like a knucklehead. Harry offered every opportunity for fence-mending, and she picketed. Yes, it stinks to do grunt work, but that's life in the working world. Vanessa should have had the maturity to shape up or ship out sooner. And while Harry did dally a bit too long, it was only out of compassion. **Where are they now?** Harry still curates at the same museum. As for Vanessa, after several months of unemployment (and analysis), she was hired by a small contemporary gallery. This time around, she kept her ego in check—and it paid off handsomely. Now she has her own assistant. Occasionally, she and Harry even meet for drinks.

And now, round three. Both our contenders hail from Baltimore, Maryland. Lynn is a twenty-eight-year-old disc jockey at a leading rock station; Josh, thirty-seven, is a radio program director. Josh, why don't you head on into the booth, while Lynn airs her story. You've got ninety seconds, Lynn—go for it!

Lynn: I began my career at an alternative music station that had a small but cultlike following. The response to my show was so strong the major stations began to notice me. Finally, a leading Top 40 radio program offered me a deal that was too sweet to refuse—they tripled my salary and gave me a slot where they said I could have creative control. They claimed they needed someone like me to make them hipper, younger, and more cutting edge.

I was completely psyched. On my first day, I submitted a playlist to my boss, Josh, who was the program director, and he thought it was terrific. For a few weeks, I was in job heaven: I was playing the music I loved, and the ratings on my show even went up a little. Josh must have come into my office four times a day, telling me what a star I was. Two months later, the problems began. I came up with the idea of doing live backstage interviews as a regular feature on my show; our listeners loved them. One night, a lead guitarist made a racist comment on the air. There was a huge uproar; we got a million outraged calls. The next morning, Josh came in and told me that the station manager had forbidden any more interview segments. Before I could protest, Josh sort of apologetically said, "Look, I wish there were something I could do, but my hands are tied. I think he's making a mistake, but we've just got to go along with this."

I decided not to kick up a fuss—after all, I was making good money, and I still had authority over my music choices, right? Wrong. A week later, Josh called me in for a meeting. He informed me the station manager thought my songs were too obscure; I had to go more mainstream. I couldn't believe it: Wasn't I hired to do exactly the opposite? Josh said, "The fact is, we're a Top 40 station, and mainstream music is what makes money. Personally, I like alternative bands, too, and if it were up to me—which it's not—I'd give you free reign. We'll figure out a way to work this out. You've got a lot of talent, and I have faith in you."

From then on, things deteriorated rapidly. I honestly tried to give my show more mass appeal, but the problem was, my idea of mainstream was Pearl Jam and theirs was Michael Bolton. I submitted playlist after playlist, only to have them nixed by the station manager. When I turned to Josh for help, he would say, "Can we talk about this later?" or make some vague comment like, "Keep plugging away." I was at sea. My energy level on the air plummeted. So did the ratings. Eventually, Josh began avoiding me, which ticked me off. Why wasn't he offering me more guidance? He was the one who hired me—why wasn't he sticking up for me? The job lasted eight months from start to finish. On my last day, Josh called in sick. I wasn't surprised.

Told in record time. We'll bring Josh out now and get his play-by-play commentary. Are you in the groove, Josh? Then rock and roll!

Josh: I'd listened to Lynn ever since her college radio-show days; I thought she was a tremendous talent. I kept telling my boss, the station manager, that we needed fresh blood—someone with their finger on the pulse of the music scene. He agreed to let me hire her.

Her show broke new ground for us. I loved it, but right up front the station manager had problems. He didn't like her music choices or her on-air personality. She was too radical for him. I asked him to give her time, to see what the audience response would be. When the ratings rose, I felt hopeful. Then, an unfortunate incident occurred during one of Lynn's live interviews. I didn't think it was such a big deal, but my boss blew his lid. He wanted to kill the show right then and there, but I pleaded for a stay of execution. Finally, he agreed to let her go on, as long as she didn't do any more interviews.

After that, the station manager just wouldn't get off my case about Lynn. She was a marked woman—he demanded that she stick strictly to Top 40 hits and sweeten up her act—basically he wanted to homogenize her. When I relayed this to her, she seemed to blame me. I didn't want to scare her by telling her I had to fight for her job, so I kept quiet and willed things to smooth over.

They didn't. I clashed so often with my boss about Lynn that I was worried for my own job. He even asked me, "Whose side are you on? Hers or mine?" I couldn't afford to be fired—I have a wife and kids—so I decided to disengage myself from the whole mess. It wasn't an easy decision to make, but Lynn wasn't a good fit for the station, and despite all my efforts, she was clearly going to lose her show. At that point, all I could do was protect myself. Even though I knew that I'd done my best, I felt so guilty and miserable I couldn't face her. We never even said goodbye.

Sad songs say so much, don't they, folks? Let's find out how the judges spin a solution.

Our turn again? Cool. **What happened here?** Interference on the airwaves. Lynn and Josh were initially attuned to each other, but the station manager caused too much static. **Then what?** Crossed wires, bad reception, whatever other radio pun you can think of. The station manager was the true trouble source: He changed the rules after everyone started playing. So Lynn wasn't allowed to do the job they hired her to do—and she blamed Josh for it. Josh was stuck between an alternative rock and a hard place; he tried to take a stand, but couldn't risk getting laid off. **Could they have turned it around?** Only if the station manager had changed his mind, retired early, or was kidnapped by terrorists. As long as he was there, Lynn and Josh were doomed. **Whose fault is it anyway?** We can't in good conscience blame Lynn—she might have been peevish at times, but the girl got rooked. Josh could have been more forthcoming, but he was helpless to change things. So it looks like we'll give Mr. Station Manager the big flip-off. **Why?** Because people in upper management should have the foresight not to hire square pegs for round holes. Because man cannot live on Bread alone. And because he's not here to defend himself. **Where are they now?** Disgusted by bureaucracy, Josh left radio for TV and is now a producer at a major video channel. Lynn went back to her old station and got promoted to program director. The station manager got kidnapped by terrorists. We wish.

Thank you, judges. For our final round, we offer you a two-for-one deal: One boss and two (count 'em), two of her disgruntled employees. Ladies and gentlemen, please put your hands together and welcome Roz, thirty-five, the manager of a magazine articles department, and two of her unhappy staff members, Ellen, twenty-eight, a senior editor and Val, twenty-seven, an associate editor . . .

Ellen: Wait a minute, wait a minute . . .

Val: El, what're you doing?

E: Hold it right there. I refuse to turn my personal career trauma into game-show fodder.

V: But what about the rolling cameras? What about the studio audience?

E: Earth to Val. There is no studio audience. It's just you and me sitting at a computer, making a handbook.

V (sadly): I know. I just wanted to prolong the illusion.

E: Don't worry; we can make more illusions later. For now, begin at the beginning. Roz was my boss for two and a half years, yours for two. And since we have to air both sides of the story, let's hear what Roz had to say.

V: Oh, well, see, there's a small problem.

E: Don't tell me you didn't call her.

V: Oh, I called her all right. My hand was shaking so bad, the phone nearly flew out of my hand. Her machine picked up; I left a message.

E: Did she call you back?

V: Oh, yes. I thought I would plotz. To my amazement, she agreed to talk and told me to call again the next week. So I did. At which point, her first words were "Val, I'm not doing this. Forget it." I tried to cajole—no dice. She said, "I don't see how there's anything in this for me. I've changed my mind and that's that." It took her six whole days to decide she wasn't "comfortable with the idea."

E: Typical Roz—she kept you waiting for a No.

V: Oh, and don't I know it. Not to be daunted, I called her second in command, one of the few people on the face of this earth who was privy to the seamy underbelly of Roz's brain. She spilled, bless her. So what we've got is Roz's side of the story, through her deputy-in-chief. Now can we go back to the game-show thing again?

E: If you insist. Do you want to walk the plank first, or should I?

V: Oh, you.

E: Fine—but only if you stifle your nervous tic of starting every Roz-related sentence with the word "Oh."

V: 'kay.

We return to our regularly broadcast show, already in progress. Ellen, you've got ninety seconds. Ready? Go!

Ellen: First, a quick background check. While Roz was making Val sweat out her morning coffee every day, I was the office darling. As long as I was polite, scraped and bowed, and, oh yeah, did my job, I was her secret weapon, her magic charm. Her words, not mine. She even glommed onto my social life, inviting herself to parties with me. She continued to dote on me until, well, until she stopped. Why, I'm not sure. Six months prior, I'd broken up with my boyfriend, and my weight dropped from going off the pill, so maybe she had a thing against ectomorphs. She told Leslie, our editor in chief—and Roz's boss—that I had an eating disorder. Curiously, she didn't fully turn on me until I started dating this cute editor at another magazine. She used to work with him and knew him, but I never could figure out why my association with him made her so sour.

Val: It's not easy being green.

E: Maybe, but—hey, butt out of my ninety seconds. All I know is that she'd begged to spend New Year's Eve with me, gave me a rave review and raise in January, and yet by early March, I was anathema. In two months, I went from pet to pestilence—without ever changing a hair. But when the worm turned, I decided not to go fishing for favors anymore. Enough was enough. A series of confrontations ensued. There was that "I am so *not* freaked out" incident we discussed earlier. Then, during one of her discourses on my bad performance, she informed me that Sam, a guy in the art department, had serious problems working with me. Dumb choice—she obviously didn't know Sam and I were tight. I said, "I find that difficult to believe, since Sam and I are good friends. Maybe we should call him in so the three of us can work out these 'problems' together." Her eyeballs pulsated for a couple of seconds, and she sputtered, "Are you saying it's a lie? Are you calling me a liar??" I said, "Roz, *liar* is such a strong word—I'd prefer to call it a gross misrepresentation." That pretty much set the tone for the rest of our days together. She went on a blind shred-fest of my work—anything with my name on it was fertilizer. If I had raised Sylvia Plath from the dead to write a story on suicide, she would've said, "Can't you find anyone who can write from experience?" I'd reached an impasse. And since I was out the door anyway, I killed time by doing the one thing that steamed Roz most: I let her know she didn't matter to me.

Thank you, Ellen. And now we'll hear Roz's side, via . . . ?

V: Roz's proxy, who requested anonymity. We'll call her Vicky, short for Victim.

Sure thing. Ladies and gentlemen, let's welcome Vicky into the studio. All set, Vic? Action!

Vicky: The whole thing began when Leslie reprimanded Roz for not producing enough. Roz got scared, so she dumped the blame on her staff—she warned certain editors to pick up the pace or else. First she spoke to Val and another editor, and the two of them responded with appropriate humility. Then she went into Ellen's office, gave the same speech, and ended by urging Ellen not to freak out since she, Roz, would nurture Ellen through this rough patch. Roz liked the notion of being Ellen's mentor. But instead of being appreciative, Ellen gave Roz attitude. According to Roz, Ellen said something like, "Freaked out? I am so *not* freaked out." Roz hated that. She couldn't stand it when people didn't show her respect—she required a certain level of obsequiousness, and Ellen wasn't putting out.

It became a battle of wills. Ellen started keeping her own hours. Taking long lunches. Calling in sick. Roz was convinced that Ellen was dicking her around, lying to her, and she had a paranoia about being lied to. Roz said Ellen was a ringleader, a troublemaker, out of control. Everyone hung out in Ellen's office, and Roz was convinced they were sitting around, saying bad things about her. She told the other editors not to fraternize with Ellen anymore. Since Roz liked surrounding herself with insecure people—it made her feel better—she viewed Ellen's natural confidence as insolence. She said Ellen was bratty, that she acted like she didn't need Roz. It bothered her that Ellen was skinny and dressed well. She said, "Ellen walks around like she's so entitled, with her nice clothes and her nice life. She expects things to come easy for her—and I'm going to make sure they don't." She used to ask, "How do I look, standing next to her?"

Most of all, Roz loved to fire people. In the course of two years, she evicted eight employees. Once she got the idea in her head, she'd circle the person, slowly put pressure on, leak bad things to Leslie. The process could take months, but she wouldn't give up until Leslie said, "Okay, fire her." It was like sex for her. This time around, Roz set her sights on Ellen. Leslie had always liked Ellen, so Roz had to campaign hard to get rid of her—she used everything she had. She said Ellen's ideas were lifeless and boring. She griped that Ellen slowed things down, let work pile up on her desk, strolled into the office at eleven o'clock. When Ellen lost weight, Roz told Leslie it was a sign of emotional instability. She kept pretending to Leslie that she was on Ellen's side: She'd say, "It's terrible, I'm doing everything I can to help her, but she won't cooperate. She has to go." Leslie had a hard time with it, but she finally agreed to put Ellen on probation. Roz was ecstatic. The day Leslie gave her the go-ahead, Roz gloated, "That little brat is going to be sorry."

Quite a chilling rendition, Vicky. So let's find out what our judges have to say about—

Ellen: WHAT? She told you not to talk to me? You never told me she told you not to talk to me! How could you not tell me she told you not to—
Val: I guess I sort of, I, I blocked it. Roz called me into her office and said, "Ellen is in trouble here, and if you know what's good for you, you'll stop hanging out in her office, or talking to her." I was pretty sure

this wasn't what good bosses do to make their employees feel safe and secure, but I didn't have the guts to argue. She wanted you in that battle alone. I'm sorry I didn't tell you before. Honest.

E: I guess it's okay. At this point, it's water under the bridge.

Vicky (interrupting helpfully): It really is. Besides, the most important thing is that you're still friends.

E: True. Even Roz couldn't ruin our friendship, no matter how hard she—hey, who asked you? You're not allowed in our dialogues. Shoo.

V: Yeah, scram. We've heard enough bad news for one chapter.

E: Not quite enough, my friend. You were the one who wanted to do this game show, remember? So now, you play, you pay.

V: Ah.

Here in the studio we have our final set of contestants. Are you comfortable, Val? Good—you're on!

Val: When I got to the magazine, I'd never been an editor before. I thought Roz would show me the ropes, but she was more interested in tying nooses. I floundered about for a month, until I became friends with Ellen. We started to write together, and that became the main focus of my job—Roz never let me edit anything, anyway. But after Ellen left, Roz started to use my lack of editing experience against me. She criticized everything I touched. I got notes on galleys that said: *If you can't edit this, please find someone who can.* She postponed my annual raise because she said I wasn't up to snuff, editing-wise. No kidding— in two years, I was only allowed to work on two features. Was I supposed to learn editing through osmosis?

Then there was the time I wrote an article about romantic movies, and even though all the other editors loved it, Roz disemboweled it. She sent it back covered with comments: *This is stupid. This is sappy. This makes me sick.* I did a rewrite, following all her specifications, and again, everyone else thought it was great. But the next morning, I saw the article listed on our schedule with *another* writer's name next to it. Without telling me, Roz had reassigned the piece to somebody else. I was humiliated.

She launched one random emotional assault after another. Once I took a freelance writer out to lunch to discuss story ideas—it was part of my job. When I submitted the expense report, Roz sent it back saying she didn't believe this guy was a legitimate writer and I would have to pay for the lunch out of my own pocket. I couldn't really afford to, so I wrote her a memo that outlined the article topics we had talked about over lunch and attached Xeroxes of stories he had written for other national magazines. It came back to my desk with a Post-it note: *I don't buy it. These ideas stink, his writing stinks—you're paying for this lunch.* She made sure I never felt anchored. She took away my assistant, made me move offices three times in six months. I would walk by her office when she was gossiping with people and hear my name through the door. I considered quitting, every single day. I went on interviews for other jobs, but they all required editing tests—my confidence was so damaged, I'd stare at the tests and think, I can't do this. I was so afraid of failing, I'd call whomever interviewed me and tell them I wasn't interested in the job after all. I stopped caring about whether I was of value to the magazine, I only thought about whether I was of value to Roz.

I had three friends at the magazine: Ellen, Sue, and Deena. Ellen decamped first; Sue got another job a month later. A month after that, Deena took maternity leave. We said goodbye on a Friday afternoon, and when she walked out of the office, I cried. I wanted to run after her, beg her not to go. I was the last person on the battlefield; I felt utterly alone in that hateful place. I didn't know what to do.

Boy, you can't make this stuff up. Take a break, Val. And while you do, we'll take a look at the flip side of the coin, as told by . . .

E: Another one of Roz's deputies whom we'll refer to as Jessica.

Fair enough. Step up to bat, Jessica, and share your story.

Jessica: Uh, I just want to remind you that these are Roz's words, not mine, okay? Okay. When it came to Val, Roz's perpetual battle cry was "Who the hell does she think she is?" She thought Val was conceited and self-promoting, that she bragged too much about all her book contracts. She called Val "a fat Jewish girl with frizzy hair who writes second-rate mystery novels."

E: All right, that's enough; there's no need for this kind of—
V: No, let her finish. I want to hear this.
E: But Val, this is ridiculous, it doesn't mean a—
V: I said, *I want to hear this.*

Jessica: Um, anyway, that was her favorite party line about Val. I remember someone once commented on how happy Val seemed one day, and Roz said, "That's because she has no self-awareness. If she knew what she was really like, and how she looked to the rest of us, she wouldn't be so happy." She rarely mentioned Val's work at all; she was more interested in dissecting her looks. She constantly joked about Val's clothes, her weight, her haircut, the way Val was so obviously cowed by authority—it gave her some sort of rush.

The day Ellen left, Roz walked into Leslie's office and said, "I think we should put Val on probation." Leslie said, "*No.* No more firings for at least six months." So Roz told us that she would merely bide her time until she could give Val the boot. She took away all of Val's work and then called her a slacker because she sat in the office with nothing to do. Her plan was to see if she could push Val to quit before the six months were up; it was like a race, a mind-fuck game. Roz told everyone she was really embarrassed to have Val on her staff, although she was the one who had hired her. She said, "Val will never be a senior editor because she's not a player. She doesn't know how to take writers to lunch and schmooze with them. She doesn't look right. She's too low-brow." Sometimes she'd watch Val walk down the hall, then turn to us and say with a slow smile, "She just doesn't get it. She'll never get it."

E: I don't get it either. **What happened here?**
V: We had a diabolically bad boss. You managed to get out while you were still emotionally whole, but I stayed long enough to become a Stockholm syn-

drome victim. She couldn't spit on you because she knew you wouldn't take it. But in my case, the crueler Roz got, the more desperately I wanted to please her. And she knew it.

E: So—**then what?**

V: I convinced myself that I somehow deserved this. Even when avenues of escape—like job interviews— became available, I wouldn't let myself take them. I thought I was at fault. Now, possibly for the first time, I see that it wasn't my fault at all. At all. And it feels pretty good.

E: Welcome back, little lamb. So to wrap up, **Could we have turned it around?** With an obscene amount of kowtowing, I might have been able to, but my knees were unwilling to withstand any more supplication. You obviously couldn't—Roz was attacking you for elements that were way beyond your control. As for **Whose fault is it anyway?**—I'll let you say it.

V: Roz's. It was Roz's fault. Roz was absolutely, positively, one-hundred-percent, swear-on-my-mother's-life, bet-the-farm-on-it wrong. She was totally, wildly, out-in-left-fieldly, cuckoo-clockily wrong. And one more thing: I am . . . *not* . . . fat!

E: Right on all counts. Finally—and this is the good part—**Where are we now?**

V: At the end of the most grueling chapter of our lives. Thanks for toughing it out with me, El. We fought the good fight together.

E: I wouldn't have wanted it any other way.

And there you have it. Hope you learned something because we sure did. For one, we found out that bosses are human, too (or at least they're on the food chain). We also realized that when you're sitting in Cineplex

Odium, it's easy to ignore the big picture. Don't forget: There are at least two takes on every story. And the more reviews you read, the better you'll understand your own role—and how your actions may affect future box-office standings. Yeah, that's the ticket. Now if we could only figure out what Vicky and Jessica are whispering about over in the corner . . . Do you think they're talking about us? Do they know anything we don't know? Should we trust them? Find out the answers to these questions and more in **Chapter Four: The Body Politic**—coming up next.

4

The Body Politic

12:20 P.M. It's been two hours since the run-in with El Cordobes. You cried yourself a small babbling brook, and you're feeling better. The snorting one means business. And unless you turn things around posthaste, that nightmare—you know, the one where you shuffle along the unemployment line, frowzy and barefoot, your sooty hands clasping the required forms in triplicate—will become a reality. You vow not to let this happen. You hate soot.

So you bust your hump for a solid hour, finishing one project and starting up another. Maybe if you do this every day—just close the door to your office and haul ass like a team of mules—you'll pull out to the front of the pack. Yeah, that's right, you'll be leader of the pack! You don't need your boss and the rest of her bullpen! You've got a set of nimble typing fingers and your very own cheddar-sharp brain. You are an island. The cheese stands alone.

Someone knocks on your door. You clear your throat and answer brightly: Come ih-hin! Enter Marnie, your best buddy in the office. An anxious look dims her usually cheerful face. You quickly assure her, "If you're worried about what happened, forget it. I'm cool." She shakes her head and takes a seat. "You know, the whole thing was Stan's fault," she whispers conspiratorially. "Cujo had no clue you were late—Joe and I were covering for you—and then Stan walks into her office and informs her you aren't in. I'm telling you, he wants that Rifkin account, and if he has to screw you over to get it, he will. He already is. You'd better watch your back."

The very thought gives you a crick in your neck. "Thanks for the warning," you say to Marnie, "but I'll be okay. I just need to haul ass like a team of mules and before you know it, I'll be leader of the pack!" Somehow it sounded better in your head, but whatever. Marnie makes clucking noises and leaves your office. You give yourself a little shake and forge ahead. Talent and hard work will win out over politicking any day. You will overcome.

Or go down trying. Smarten up, sister: Idealism only works in the kind of movies that get colorized. Off-camera, politics are the foundation of corporate America.

Now, you might be thinking, "What in the Sam Hill do Val and Ellen know? Like they're making a million dollars a year? I'll concentrate on doing a good job and everything will be peachy." Well, chew on this: "Idealists think that playing politics is a form of cheating," says Adele Scheele, Ph.D., a psychologist who specializes in career issues. "But the truth is, if you ignore the goings-on at the office, you'll die. If you ignore your boss and fail to build a relationship with her, she'll think you're not smart or that you don't care about your job. She might think you're against her. And then you'll be overlooked come promotion time—no matter how excellent your work might be. Of course, the ultimate formula is to do good work *and* to develop a strong relationship with the boss. But if you can't do both, choose the latter. The number one requirement of any job is make your boss comfortable."

Sure, someone with a fancy-schmancy graduate degree says it, and you lap it up like Snack-Pack pudding. In any case, the scary part is that strategically trying to break down your office might give you an office breakdown. Almost everyone agrees: Keeping up with the jackals can be a losing battle. What with all the mind-bending machinations, you end up feeling overwhelmed, undermined, and bad all over. As such, rather than further entrenching—and depressing—you with an infusion of CIA tactics, we've decided to drum up a few ways you can actually make yourself feel better. Frankly, we couldn't give a possum's patoot what color your parachute is—we're more interested in a comfy fit.

So, try this on for size: One of the main frustrations of office campaigning is that your success is contingent on other people. It's a big, fat—all together now—codependent process. Subsequently, we propose a two-pronged approach. Prong #1: Know thy neighbor. Prong #2: Help thyself. Okay, maybe they're more like commandments than prongs, but that's beside the point. In any case, our theory is that an office is like a machine, with every person providing an essential function. To understand the mechanics truly, you need to learn how each component/colleague operates—and then figure out how to make the whole megillah work for you.

Where to start? The instruction manual, of course. And gracious, we just happen to have one right here.

la machinator X101 ("The ultimate in office machines"): A user's guide.

Congratulations—you are now the proud owner of **la machinator**—the ultimate in office machines. Your new **la machinator** is the product of sophisticated political technology and is engineered to the highest corporate standards. To ensure its peak performance, please read the following instructions carefully and keep them in your desk for quick reference. Or dial our 1-800-4-**lamach** hot line for your servicing needs. WELCOME TO THE **la machinator** FAMILY!

PARTS AND ASSEMBLY
1. The Predator

Function: To sabotage other people on her way to the top
Fuel: Jealousy and envy
Standard features: Intent to harm. The Predator is not merely competitive, she's bloodthirsty. Your wins are her losses—conversely, her victories must result in your defeat. She reacts to other people's successes like poison ivy—they make her inflamed and rash. Which creates a scratchy situation.
Operating instructions: Watch your back—but not to the point of whiplash. "Just because someone's out to get you, doesn't mean you can be gotten," says Dr. Judith Sills. "Assess her goals, and guard against them. Does she actually pose a threat to your job, or is she just

socially disruptive? Get a realistic picture." Next, she advises, mobilize your allies. On this type of social battlefield, you're wise to gather your troops. "Apprise your friends of the situation," says Dr. Sills. "Tell them, 'Jane Doe is saying this about me—what do you think I should do?' You may be able to find safety in numbers." Finally (and this is the tough part) you'll have to face the enemy. Accrue solid evidence—you can't confront her unless you have the goods. The gist of your message: *I see what you're doing, and I know who you are. Although you obviously feel more comfortable talking behind my back, I'm capable of a more direct approach.* "Don't get sidetracked discussing who said what to whom," warns Dr. Sills. "You shouldn't help her discover who her leaks are. Keep your cool, and make her realize she can't shake you. You're allowed to stand up to a bully."

Utility: The Predator forces her peers to be more alert and efficient. If she only knew . . .

2. The Transmitter

Function: To gather, process, and broadcast office information (a.k.a. gossip)

Fuel: Interpersonal drama, low self-esteem

Standard features: Unlike The Predator, The Transmitter doesn't want to hurt you personally (although if somebody else does, you can count on her to pass it on). She can become deeply attached to and involved with the lives of her colleagues (she's a "people person!"). Ideally, she'd like to be the center of those lives, but if that's not possible, she'll make do on the fringe. She needs to be needed (she's a "needy Nellie!"); being recognized as The Source makes her feel important. Interloping gives her an adrenaline high. Yes, she may be an annoying busybody, but in her mind she's just being nurturing (she's a "Mommy bear!"). Besides which, she's got great dirt.

Operating instructions: Let she who has never dished dirt cast the first mud pie. "Jobs are not all about pushing paper," says Dr. Sills. "They're about interacting within a self-contained society, too. Face it: We all enjoy gossip—except when it's about us. Sure, you can tsk-tsk a gossiper, but the receivers are as much at fault. Since gossip can be a guilty pleasure, it's easier to blame someone else for it. So the broadcaster gets the bad rep, and you just reap the benefits." Subsequently, when you're dealing with The Transmitter, you should be aware of your own participation. You've got two choices here: Tune in and shut up—or turn off and drop out. You don't have to be a part of the grapevine if you don't want to be. However, getting the juice can be an important factor in fitting into the office infrastructure. Just remember: It's always better to receive than to give. Finally, if you've caught wind of gossip that could potentially damage you, Dr. Sills suggests you head directly to The Transmitter. Do not pass Go, do not collect two hundred outside opinions. "Firmly but pleasantly remark, 'I heard you said the boss hates me. What's the story?' Odds are, she'll disclose and you can use that information to your advantage. By and large, her two favorite words are *'Tell me!'* All you have to do is ask."

Utility: Says Dr. Sills, "Every organization needs informal channels of information. Because formal communication can be spotty, you have to rely on informal exchanges." So don't hate her because she's knowledgeable (but feel free to hate her because she's beautiful).

3. The Latcher

Function: To grab on—and never let go
Fuel: An insatiable need for attention. All the fucking time.
Standard features: This girl's the Ever-present Bunny: She keeps clinging and clinging and clinging and clinging ... She may be having job problems and thus overcompensates by trying to improve her social situation. Unfortunately, the more "improving" she does, the more you want to douse her with bug repellent. Another possibility: She sees work as a way to make friends she's unable to make elsewhere. And you just happen to be in the right place, at all the wrong times.
Operating instructions: Set boundaries. Good fences make good neighbors. "It's not easy to say no," says Dr. Sills, "but practice. Your mission in the office isn't to make yourself crazy to avoid hurting someone else's feelings. All you can do is treat others decently, set limits so they don't get in your face—and not feel bullied or overreact to their anger or pain." To cushion the blow, cut back slowly. Start by having lunch thrice a week instead of every day. After a month, make it once or twice a week. Continue your reduction plan until you've reached your goal date: once in a blue moon. If, however, your Latcher is the sort who wants exclusive rights on your time, you'll probably have to say something (nicely). Dr. Sills recommends: "Mary and I are going to lunch on Tuesday. Obviously, I'd invite you, except we're meeting to discuss that project for next month. But please don't think we're trying to exclude you—it's just business." If she freaks, she freaks. You're her colleague, not her nanny, so save the guilt for a rainy day.

Utility: Makes you look popular. Hey, it's better than nothing.

4. The Refrigerator

Function: To give you—and everyone else—the cold shoulder

Fuel: Excessive shyness, reclusiveness, Freon, liquid nitrogen, *no hablo Inglés* . . . who knows? (Or *¿quíen sabe?*) She's not talking.

Standard features: By all accounts, The Refrigerator is seen as being cold, withdrawn, distant, unfriendly. Over time, this has caused everyone to conclude she's a snooty-ass-bitch-whore-douchebag. Whether or not she deserves this reputation is up for grabs. She may merely be painfully timid, awkward, or socially inept. Or not. Who knows? She's not talking.

Operating instructions: Quoth Dr. Sills: "You have to judge people by your own standards. Do you personally know she's an ice princess, or did someone [that would be The Transmitter] tell you? The notion that everyone has to be warm and fuzzy is wrong: This is America, she can be unfriendly if she chooses. And if her unfriendliness is bothering you so much, you might want to figure out why. Is it because you need to be the focus of her attention [that would be The Latcher]? Does her cool self-assurance make you want to knock her down a peg or two [that would be The Predator]? Think about it. In the meantime, your only recourse is to be your usual friendly self [that would be your usual friendly self]. When you're walking down the hall, say 'Hello!' If she doesn't respond, so be it."

Utility: Provides mystery, intrigue, and gives everyone

else a chance to speculate about her. Friend, foe—who knows? She's not talking. So the rest of you might as well.

5. The Defensive Linebacker

Function: To keep you off her turf

Fuel: One part self-preservation, one part fear, two-parts defensiveness, and one part paranoia. Her engine's running on super-unleaded sensitivity.

Standard features: She's a guarder, a charter, a midnight martyr. She wears her heart on her feet—and people are constantly stepping on her toes. Her territorial tendencies may stem from past burns, fear of firing, blazing ambition, heated possessiveness, whatever. Cross her line, and she'll combust.

Operating instructions: Yes, it's that old, "setting boundaries" thing again. Or rather, negotiating new ones. Assuming you aren't purposely romping on her stomping grounds, or planning a hostile takeover, you'll have to come up with some sort of peace treaty. "In many jobs, there are gray zones where employees' responsibilities overlap," says Dr. Sills. "This is where conflicts start. Instead of staging a power struggle, you need to figure out a way to work together." How, pray tell? "Put aside your anger and schedule a summit meeting," advises Dr. Sills. "Begin with, 'I think you and I have a problem—not between us personally, but in terms of delineating our job assignments. I know it's only because we both care about our work. In light of this, I'm sure we can find a way to establish a satisfactory division of labor.'" Then, whip out your trusty pad of paper and start dividing. If necessary, arrange to meet every week to discuss your progress, so all activities remain aboveboard. Make it clear that you're her ally, not her opponent. And as a last resort, you might ask Mom or Dad (i.e., your boss) to settle the dispute. Preferably, though, you'll act like adults and settle it yourselves. Might we suggest paper, scissors, rock?

Utility: Keeps people in their respective places. Defines everyone's role, and in the process, ensures that the office machine runs like . . .

. . . the *ultimate* office machine—la one, la only, **la machinator!** Now that you're familiar with the equipment, it's time to kick it into high gear. Which brings us back to Prong #2 (that would be Help thyself). The theme song here: "One." You're going for that singular sensation. The concept being: a certain amount of independent strategic planning can minimize your frustration, maximize your control. So before you start playing Twister with the gang, do some solo footwork. Below, a few friendly (and maybe a touch sneaky) workplace tips that you can follow, all by your lonesome. They're safe, easy to implement, and may just give you enough of an edge to make your life a little lovelier, a whole lot shinier. And that's a nice reflection on you.

IF YOU FEED THEM, THEY WILL COME.

Gossip equals information. Information equals power. Power equals money. Money equals comfort; comfort equals shoes that don't pinch; shoes that don't pinch equal . . . (dammit, Jim, we're writers, not mathematicians!). So what's information again? Oh yeah, power. Which is what this chapter's all about.

According to Dr. Scheele, "The exchange of information happens during lunch, before and after meetings, at drinks after work, at coffee breaks, in elevators, and yes, even at the proverbial water cooler." Sure, but between personal calls and more personal calls, who has time to scurry around to all these locales, burrowing around for acorns of gossip? Not us, we'll tell you that for free. Easier to lure your coworkers into your office and then stall them such that they drop a few info-nuggets your way. How? Two words: squirrel bait. Some of our favorite brands:

- *Candy.* For optimal results, put out sweets that don't travel well: No stay, no pay. Goodies that melt in their mouths and their hands are preferable—you want them to linger long enough to feel that sugar rush and unload a few secrets. A jar of Gummy Bears is the best choice—too sticky to hold, too yummy to eat just one. Unwrapped chocolates (e.g., Milk Duds and Junior Mints) are also fine fare. Be attuned to public preferences. Is this a nuts or no-nuts crowd? Thumbs up or down on white chocolate? Then shop accordingly.

- *Snacks.* Popcorn tops the list here—it's popular even with diet mavens and not as greasy or crumbly as chips and cookies. In predominantly female offices, rice cakes and pretzels are good options as well. Whatever you do, don't let supplies run out. No swill, no spill—in order to build a reputation as the local refreshment stand, you have to maintain a steady stock.

- *Beverages.* This requires an office fridge (and if you don't have one, it could be a good investment). Cheap bottled water and a couple six-packs of soda should do the trick. Again, get a gauge of office favorites. Even if you're strictly a Classic Coke girl, keep some diet quenchers on hand for weight watchers—in these calorie-conscious times, no Tab, no blab.

- *Vanities.* A full-length mirror on the back of your door can be a powerful enticement. While you're at it, throw in a hairbrush, hairspray, and other assorted beauty aids to prolong loitering time—no mousse, no juice. Don't forget the clear nail polish for those unexpected snags. And a can or two of Static Guard (unscented, please) is always a plus during those dry winter months.

- *Supplies.* Aspirin, breath mints, tampons, spray deodorant, paper towels, change for vending machines, stamps, cold medicine, Band-Aids, vitamin C, tissues, Sweet 'n Low, wrapping paper, ribbon, Tums, emery boards, hand lotion, batteries—the list goes on (and if all else fails, you can open a pharmacy). She who gives also receives. With a minimum of effort, you'll look resourceful, prepared, helpful, and generous—and your greedy coworkers will never even realize you're making them sing for their supper. No pain, big gain.

Drop-In Box

Of course, shepherding the flock into your office is only half the battle. Once they're there, you've got to find a way to make them bleat. Ten good opening lines:

1. What a beautiful day! Kind of makes me feel like, I don't know, *talking*!
2. Coffee?
3. Paul, I just want you to know that whatever happens between you and Karen, I'm on your side.
4. The great thing about you is the way you describe situations in such *detail*. It's a real gift.

5. Cigarette?
6. Karen, I just want you to know that whatever happens between you and Paul, I'm on your side.
7. You know, I feel like you're the only person around here I can trust.
8. Back rub?
9. Can you believe this whole Paul and Karen thing? Whatever happens, I refuse to get involved.
10. Don't worry—your little expense-account secrets are safe with me.

BE AN EQUAL OPPORTUNITY KISSER.

Oh, we could drone on about the importance of making nice with the boss, but as far as we're concerned, that's yesterday's mashed potatoes. Anyone with half a brain (which sums up roughly a third of the work force) knows well enough to kiss up. Whole-brained employees give more extensive lip service. They kiss down. They kiss sideways. They make like oscillating fans and give multidirectional blow jobs.

Which is as it should be. Good things don't just come from on high. The air down there is rife with opportunity. Keep it clear with a generous helping of sugar smacks, beginning with . . .

• *Your assistant.* If you're lucky enough to have an assistant, don't abuse the privilege. That person sitting outside your office isn't simply an envelope licker. On the contrary: She's a spin-doctor, backup artist, damage controller, news source, all-around indispensable ally who just happens to lick envelopes, too. If you look out for her, she'll look out for you. It's that simple.

How to win her allegiance? Common courtesy, respect, and personal hygiene are always good places to start. This means you don't send her on frivolous errands, make her the brunt of your weird hormonal jags, or fart in her general direction. But why stop there? Ask about her life; act like you really care. Remember her boyfriend's name. Pick up her phone if she's not there. Bring *her* a cup of coffee, if you (god forbid) get in before she does. Introduce her as someone who works *with* you, not *for* you. Look, she's getting paid a fraction of your salary to do your dirty work. The least you can do is take off your shoes when she's mopping.

Still, these are merely fundamentals in the care and feeding of a valuable assistant. She likes you? Great—now go the extra mile and make her adore you. Show your appreciation by giving her birthday and Christmas presents (nice ones—not some dumb paperback you happened to pick up in the drugstore). Take her out to lunch. Bring her trinkets from business trips; leave flowers on her desk when she's having a bad day. Money can't buy you love? Not a problem—we'll settle for a short-term lease.

Finally—and this is key—help advance your assistant's career. Fact: Every underling in the world is eager to move up. If you give her a boost, she'll be eternally grateful, i.e., useful. Don't limit her to administrivia: Ask for her input, increase her responsibilities, recommend her for nongruntesque projects, and then call attention to her good work. Keep her apprised of any possible job openings, help her with her résumé, and offer to be a reference (provided you can rave in good conscience). In doing so, you'll make her feel you're on her side. This, correspondingly, puts her on your side—which is precisely where you want her to be.

Of course, in black and white, it all sounds far more Machiavellian than it really is. You'd probably do all this out of the goodness of your heart anyway, right? *Bien sûr*. Which moves us right along to . . .

- *The other assistants (especially your boss's)*. There are very few secrets a support staff isn't privy to. After all, these are the people who type personal letters, file confidential documents, open mail, eavesdrop on phone conversations, monitor the flow of office traffic, and so on. If you win their trust and affection, they might cut you in on their wealth of knowledge. So make like a tandoori chicken and curry—favor, that is. No grand gestures necessary; basic friendliness and a few well-placed compliments should do the trick. Since assistants are commonly treated like mindless carrier pigeons, you'll get points just by regarding them as evolved mammals. Bear in mind, however, that your own assistant comes first—if she turns on you, the rest of the flock could follow.

- *The back office crew*. Messengers, mailroom workers, cafeteria people, cleaning staff, security guards, cashiers, repairmen—you name 'em, you need 'em. The day your boss suddenly wants a ceiling mirror installed in his private shower is the day your friendship with Chet the handyman pays off in spades

- *Anyone new*. First impressions can be profitable. Office neophytes are scared and vulnerable as hell. Have mercy on them. Be a one-woman welcome wagon. Invite the new hires to lunch or drinks; offer to show them the ropes. They'll always see you as the nice person who showed them how to cadge office supplies—and will forever, subconsciously, be in your debt. The more allies you have, the better. Since you never know when you'll need to call in some chits, you might as well pucker up for safety, early on.

One final comment on the subject: Don't feel conscience-stricken for pandering. Bootlicking is an art form; like painting and dancing, it has its own integrity. Complimenting your boss's new topiary haircut isn't deception, it's good etiquette. Still not convinced? Then let's try this quick group activity: Raise your hand if you've ever faked an orgasm. Okay, you can all put your hands down. When you faked that orgasm, did you do it with malicious intent? Mercy, no. You probably did it (a) to make your partner feel like God's gift and (b) so you could get some sleep already. Honorable objectives both. So the next time you're face-to-butt with your boss, approach it like you're simulating the big O. Make all the right sounds ("I love this job, it feels so good, oh god, this job is incredible"). Make all the right moves (appear responsive and aroused, be flexible, participate with gusto). Skip the excessive theatrics and keep it simple (releasing a small, breathless moan speaks volumes more than thrashing around like a freshwater bass on a hook). Bosses—like bedfellows—*want* to believe the charade, so you won't have to do too much convincing. When you're done, your boss will feel like she's God's gift. And you'll sleep better for it.

DEVELOP SPECIAL SKILLS.

In the workplace, aptitude in the three R's is academic, not to mention way low in dazzle potential. Anyone can put together a complete sentence or calculate a 15 percent tip—what you need are talents that'll make you stand out in the crowd. It's like being a doctor: The more you subspecialize, the less the real work you have to do and the more money you make. In fact, it's better than being a doctor because if the computer file you're trying to save for a coworker dies, odds are she'll still appreciate your effort, as opposed to bitterly blaming you and then hitting you with a malpractice suit. But let's not get ahead of ourselves. Some particularly good party tricks to keep up your sleeve:

- *Repairs and maintenance.* Yeah, yeah, the whole office can slap together a spread sheet in their sleep, but does anyone know how to replace the toner in the Xerox machine? Or call up the print queue on the computer? Or change their voice-mail messages for that matter? Make these scary technological niceties your business. Office machinery is built to break, so if you're user-friendly, you'll be on the A (for All-but-indispensable) list. People will like you. More important, they'll learn to depend on you. Added perk: As the local fix-it, you'll catch glimpses of your colleagues' computer screens, projects, and correspondence, thus obtaining inside information. And we all know what information is.

- *Paper-train yourself.* A lot of good dirt gets put in writing—and with a bit of practice, you can access it all. Learn to read upside-down (for those times you're standing on the other side of someone's document-littered desk), at the speed of light (for those times you're standing by the printer and something interesting scrolls out), and know whose handwriting is whose (for those times you "accidentally" come upon unsigned, personal interoffice notes). Moreover, study your boss's chicken scratch until you can decode it instantly, the dream scenario being:

Colleague (thrusting hieroglyphics on your boss's letterhead in front of your face): Can you read this? I just can't make it out.

You: It says you should give me your company credit cards, the keys to your corner office, and that green Armani jacket you wore last Tuesday.

Colleague: Oh. Okay. Here.

• *Load up your memory bank.* Being able to rattle off all your workmates' extensions will elicit immediate respect. Producing other commonly used four-digit combinations (the mailroom, personnel, the benefits office, the cash window, etc.) on command will add an element of fear. Top off the list with phone numbers for local food-delivery joints, car services, florists, and the time and weather, and people will think you're like a genius. Hey, number stuff impresses people.

Furthermore, keep a calendar of important dates: Birthdays, anniversaries, vacation schedules, paid holidays. If you're the only one who remembers to utter those six little words ("Oh, by the way, happy birthday") you'll look awfully good. Piece of cake.

ASK FIRST.

This one's short and sweet. Almost every boss we spoke to craved the lilty, curly sound of a question mark at the end of her employee's sentences. Bosses want supplication (don't they get nosebleeds sitting on such high horses?). And as pathetic as this little power ploy may be, it's an easy requirement to satisfy. Before you speak up in a meeting, ask, "Could I make a suggestion?" Before you enter your boss's office, ask, "Is it okay to come in?" Before you stand up and flush, ask "Do you mind if I wipe?" And so on.

MAKE CONCESSIONS.

There's this old joke:

A grade-school teacher tells her students, "Okay, class, today we're going to have a contest. Whoever can name the greatest man in the world will win a prize." Kid in the front row raises his hand and says "Abraham Lincoln." Teacher replies, "Well . . . yes, Abraham Lincoln was a very great man, but he wasn't the greatest man in the world." Little girl with pigtails raises her hand and says, "Martin Luther King." Teacher answers, "Well . . . Martin Luther King was certainly a great, great man—but he wasn't the greatest man in the world." From the back of the room, a little boy with glasses waves his hand and calls out, "Jesus Christ." Teacher claps her hands and exclaims, "That's exactly right! Jesus Christ was the greatest man in the world! Now come up here and collect your prize." Boy walks up and as he's taking the prize, teacher looks at him and says, "Little Martin Weinstein—how did *you* know that Jesus Christ was the greatest man in the world?" To which the kid replies, "Actually, Teacher, *everyone* knows that *Moses* was the greatest man in the world. But business is business."

So young, yet so wise. We couldn't have said it better ourselves, Marty. Business *is* business—it has little to do with your personal code, moral or otherwise. It is not a barometer of your worth as a human being. Accordingly, when it comes to differences of opinion in the workplace, don't bother holding your ground until you're buried in it—you'll only dig up trouble. Better to concede and win than to lose your shirt over something dumb like principle. As someone once said (we think it was Kenny Rogers, but maybe it was Michael Jordan's shrink), you gotta know when to fold 'em. Know when to walk away. KNOW WHEN TO RUN . . . oh, never mind.

This is especially true in less-subjective situations, situations in which you've (knock wood a thousand times) actually made a mistake. Every smart cookie slips up from time to time. Shrewd cookies have the good sense to apologize. According to Dr. Scheele, "If you really bungle, it's going to get back to you anyway. Admit to your boss that you messed up. Say, 'I feel terrible. Here's what happened. Tell me if I can do anything to repair it or lessen the repercussions. I'm sorry, and it won't happen again.'" Abjection sustained.

Furthermore, after you've discussed your error, put a lid on it—drop it and move on. "Talking about the error is like picking a scab," says one wise manager we know. "No boss needs to be reminded of how you messed up; she'd rather forget about it, too. In the meantime, stay out of your boss's hair. You need to give her a chance to get to like you again—and she won't if you're in her face apologizing every two seconds. Try staying late and coming in early for a few weeks. It sounds obvious, but it conveys the message that you want to keep your job. If I get the sense that someone is trying to make up for a mistake, I'll always wipe the slate clean."

We're talking prostration nation. Are you equal to the challenge? Take this quiz and see.

Question 1: You know you shouldn't have done (*insert your mistake here*), and you want to make it right. You:

a. Blame that bitch Sandi from promotions. Anyone who dots their i's with hearts deserves to take the heat.

b. Shake with fear until the bonding on your teeth chatters off.
c. Shrug it off. What're they gonna do, cane you?
d. Contemplate major plastic surgery and a change of identity. Decide not to take the easy way out; confess instead.
e. Think to yourself, It all happened so quickly, I must have dreamed it. Of course. It was all . . . a bad . . . zzzzzzz.

Passing the buck is a bad idea: What goes around, comes around. And fear and denial are rarely productive emotions. If you circled C, you're on the right track. Otherwise, it might be time to take that interview suit to the cleaners.

Question 2: Your boss found out what you did and she's livid. You're never seen her so pissed. You:

a. Tell her you're sorry, but you can't think straight when you've got monster cramps.
b. Tell her you're sorry and beg for forgiveness on bended knee. While you're down there, reach out, grab her legs, and never let go.
c. Tell her you're sorry, and, if it would make her feel better, she should go ahead and slap you silly, just slap you into next week, slap, slap, slap, the way Mom used to do before Dad took her to "the nice place where people rest."
d. Tell her you're sorry, then shrug and say with a grin, "What're you gonna do, ground me?"
e. Tell her you're sorry, let her rant, and steer clear until she cools to a low simmer.

Trotting out that old "time of the month" excuse again? Get original. Unless you work at a women's magazine, answer A will only put a cramp in your upward mobility. If you circled B, let go of her legs—c'mon, that's right, you can do it—and get a grip on your sanity. As for C and D, your boss is not your parent; if you relate to her as such, you'll be treated like a child in return. E's the way to go, hands down.

Question 3: Your boss hurled blowtorches at you for an hour. Everyone else must notice your singed eyebrows because they're avoiding you. As the new office pariah, you:

a. Corner Sandi in the back bathroom stall and hiss satanically, "I bet you think this is pretty funny, huh? Well, go ahead and have your little joke. One of these days, when you least expect it, I'll have the last laugh! Yes! I will! AHHH ha ha ha ha ha . . . !"
b. Go around to your coworkers saying, "Be friends with me?"
c. Ride it out. They need you as much as you need them.
d. Sit under your desk, rocking and twitching.
e. Shrug defiantly. What're they gonna do—as if you care!

Working in an office requires a certain sickening amount of teamwork. You can't function as a single unit—if you could there'd be a 100 million microcorporations cleaning up all over America. Better to keep your distance for a day or two. Let things settle down. Then approach your colleagues and try to thaw things out by being your normal, friendly self. In short, skip the histrionics, brush that chip off your shoulder, and go for C.

Question 4: It's been a few days since D(isaster) Day. Your colleagues are filtering back into your office to hang out. Even your boss poked her head in to say hello this morning. The world is partly sunny again. You:

a. Pray things'll hold steady. You can't type with your fingers crossed for much longer.
b. Feel cocky and start making noises about "that raise that's coming to me."
c. Shrug scornfully—what're they gonna do, risk losing "the best damn catcher the department softball team ever had?"
d. Live in fear that you'll make another major mistake. Since you're too paralyzed to work, you pass the days smearing Elmer's glue on your hand, waiting for it to dry and peeling it off.
e. Have your assistant go out and buy flowers for your boss with a card that reads, "Happy to begin again with you!"—and while she's at it, she can throw in a bunch for herself.

A few days? That's just not enough time to build up trust again—two or three weeks is more like it. What's more, you've got to be a pretty shiny penny to be demanding raises, so why don't you wait for your yearly review (and until then, get to work). And whatever you do, don't buy your boss flowers unless it's her birthday—and never send your assistant on personal errands. They'll both hate you for it. Your best bet is A.

Question 5: Things have never fully recovered since the screwup. You've had some major projects taken away, and your long-distance phone calls are being checked by accounting. It doesn't look good. You:

a. Smear. Dry. Peel. Smear. Dry. Peel.
b. Leave a pamphlet for MCI Friends and Family on your boss's desk.
c. Start glad-handing your way around the office—shaking hands, kissing babies, passing out cigars—to rustle up support.
d. Quit in a huff.
e. Shrug it off—what are they gonna do, fire you?

Possibly. Put down the Elmer's, and listen up: At this point, trying to score popularity points is bootless. Like rats, your coworkers are more apt to jump away from a sinking ship than to rally around it. The MCI package is a nice idea except those vipers around you hardly qualify as either friends or family. Furthermore, doing anything in a huff is dusty and often regrettable. The fact is, if your workload is thinning and your phone calls are being monitored, you've got a spot of trouble on your hands. The situation is bleak. You never imagined such horror—even in your worst dreams. Or did you? Does your id know something your ego doesn't? Has it been trying to warn you all this time? For a quick dip into the sea of your unconscious, go directly to **Nightmare on Work Street**, *a.k.a.* **Chapter Five**. *In the meantime, the correct response here: None of the above. (Okay, so it was a trick question. What're you gonna do, sue us?)*

How Low Will You Go?

And we don't mean limbo dancing. To measure your threshold of gain, we did a political survey of fifty women at work. While the readings varied, we found that the majority of you could hold your heads high and proclaim, "I may have lied and cheated, but I've never killed for pleasure!" Mazeltov. Below, some specifics on the claws and effect:

• When asked about **lying on your résumé,** 50 percent of you admitted to crying *summa cum wolf.* Many of your deceptions centered around wordplay: One woman claimed she had "made" several sales presentations, when, in truth, she had only attended them (okay, so maybe she "made" it to them on time). Another woman "researched" projects instead of proofreading them. Other falsehoods involved number-crunching (e.g., graduating college in four years instead of six; fiddling with dates of employment to avoid explaining downtime). Inflation was also common (e.g., puffing up a small freelance project into a high-level assignment). And a few people went so far as to create fictional jobs and fancy titles for themselves or claim false contacts with bigwigs in their industry. Our personal favorite: The woman who saw Steven Spielberg in a restaurant and put him down as a reference. Talk about swindler's list.

• Currying favor was another popular pastime. Sixty percent of you resorted to **spending personal time or resources to win points with your boss.** Methods included buying flowers for a boss's birthday, baby-sitting pets and children, plant-sitting, uh, plants, running errands on weekends, lending clothes or makeup, fixing a superior up on dates, serving as a chaperone at various parties and events, exercising with a boss, entertaining a boss's spouse, and/or being a personal gift shopper. Whew. With all this extracurricular activity, who has time to hold down a job?

• Seventy-five percent of you also confessed to **playing**

up your importance on a successful project. One ad copywriter told us about a campaign with which she was only marginally involved. "It ended up being a huge success—and I guess I wanted some glory," she said. "Every time someone mentioned how fabulous it was, I'd say, 'Yeah, thanks—we all worked so hard on it; I'm just glad it paid off.' Maybe it wasn't the most honorable thing to do, but it's not like I said I single-handedly created the whole campaign, right?" Right. More or less. Similarly, 40 percent of you were culpable of **accepting credit where none was due.** As one marketing consultant told us, "My boss kept asking me about a particular sales projection. Although I wasn't working on it, I knew all the figures because my office mate was in charge of the whole thing. So, I'd give my boss the info. To this day, I think my boss believes I was responsible for the report." Guilty as charged.

- Curiously, when asked about **diverting blame onto someone else,** a paltry 25 percent answered in the affirmative. The primary motive: To thine own ass be true. "I wouldn't blame someone I knew well," a publicist hastened to qualify. "That would be a betrayal. I would—and have—however, used people outside the office as bad cops in order to keep my record clean." Just like her conscience. *Nyet.*

- By and large, although you weren't eager to accuse the innocent, most of you felt free to malign them. A whopping 90 percent of you indulged in **badmouthing your coworkers, often to your own advantage.** Why? "If we didn't gossip and talk about each other, I don't know how we'd fill the day," observed one assistant trader. On a more Machiavellian level, "Informing others that there's a slacker in your midst will only make you look better in comparison," said a paralegal. The question being: In comparison to what?

- On a more reassuring note, only 10 percent of you stooped to **stealing someone else's work**. Pride was a big crime preventer: "If you have to plagiarize, it's like admitting you have no talent," said one magazine editor. Actual transgressions were generally on a small scale. One strategic planner overheard her colleagues brainstorming and promptly used their ideas in a presentation she gave to her boss. "It was kind of dirty," she allowed, "But no one ever knew." Oh, then that makes it all okay.

- Going from the basement to the sewer, in terms of **sabotaging someone's work**, 4 percent of you pleaded guilty. The most common undermining routes: Erasing computer files and voice-mail messages and purposely "forgetting" to tell coworkers about important deadlines or meetings. Since we don't like to be judgmental, we won't say anything (except that we think this kind of behavior sucks meat).

Finally, in the Land of What If?, for double your salary, would you . . .

Get someone else fired to save your own skin? Twenty percent said yes. One respondent who'd already done the dirty deed said, "In my entire professional history, this is the one act I'm most ashamed of. I had to inform on a colleague or get in deep shit with the boss. I squealed like a pig. I was a coward." Listen and learn.

Blackmail a boss to advance? Only 12 percent of our respondents said they'd attempt such risky business. The one woman who'd actually done so in the past said, "I still don't consider it blackmail—it was more like insinuation. My boss had padded her expense account—and I found out. I'd been passed over for a promotion twice; a month before my annual review, I looked straight at my boss and made a veiled reference about 'creative accounting.' I'm not positive she got the implication, but either way, I was promoted. To me, that was all that mattered." Chacun à son priorities.

Sleep with the boss to get ahead? As it were. Though a number of our respondents had bedded with bosses for romantic reasons, only one woman did it for professional gain. "I was in medical school," she said. "The chief surgeon always flirted with me. Around the time of my 'match' (when fourth-year students compete for a limited number of jobs in their chosen field), he offered to give me a complete physical, pelvic exam and all. I agreed— and got my match. And maybe I'm rationalizing, but it's not like we had sex." Point taken. Even so, we're not convinced that letting someone stick a cold speculum in your code of honor is the best way to ensure a healthy reputation. Granted, morality is in the eye of the perpetrator. But don't fool yourself: No matter how well you conceal your dirty laundry, your true colors will come out in the wash.

5

Nightmare on Work Street

1:34 P.M. *Rumble, rumble.* You're staring at your computer screen, deep in thought, when a loud noise suddenly breaks your concentration. *Rumble, rumble.* What the—? Did Marnie rent a Sherman tank for your long-planned office coup? *Glug, glug, glug.* No such luck—it's only your stomach. Even animals in captivity need a meal every now and then.

You run down to the corner deli, grab a turkey sandwich, two Diet Cokes, and a six-pack of Oreos and head back to your cage. Feeding time. Panting slightly, you plop down at your desk, unwrap your goodies, and . . . sonofabitch—you said *no tomatoes!* Uch. Still, the food slides down with considerable ease. Gosh, you were hungry. That morning maelstrom really stoked your appetite.

Now, back to work—but first, your eyes could use a little rest. You lean waaaay back in your chair. That turkey was swell, wasn't it? Tryptophan slowly seeps into your brain. Incredible as it sounds, you feel relaxed. In fact, you're feeling pretty fine. Yes sir, yessireebob, you're drifting a little, you're feeling kind of dozy . . . you're . . . you're . . .

Running through a forest, running through a forest, BANG! you run into a tree. A giant wolf is chasing you and *she wants blood!* Glancing back in terror through the dank, greenish light, you can *see* her glinty fangs, *hear* her rasping snarls, *smell* her deadly scent, *feel* her fiery breath, *taste* the acrid fear in your, BANG! you run into a tree! Your legs are made of water; your feet are filled with sand; she's catching up, she's opening her jaws, she's, BANG! you run into a tree, *she's going to eat you alive!* You frantically look at your watch—9:14—and, oof, trip over an enormous coffee maker, stumbling, tumbling . . . The giant bull is right on top of you now, her snorts are getting louder, she's—hey, what's your high school social studies teacher doing here?—about to shred you under her sharp cloven hooves, filet you like a fish! You try to scream for help, but the air is so thick with soot, your throat closes up. "Squeak!" you gasp desperately, "Squeak, squeak!" No one can hear you! *You are all alone!* Burrowing frantically into the ground, you curl into a tight ball, pull your red cape over your head, and cry and cry and cry and cry . . .

There, there, it's all right. You don't know it yet, but you're having a bad dream. In a few moments, you'll wake up and realize that you're not running in a forest after all. No, no, you're actually sitting at your desk, head tipped back, mouth wide open, safe and secure in your own little—

AAAGHHHH! AAAGHHH! AAAGHHH!

Nothing like a choice between the frying pan and the

fire, eh? In Job Hell, even sleep offers no respite. As if working in a demonic office isn't torture enough, at night, when you fall into bed, the nightmare often continues. For good reason. Experts agree that sleep "life" parallels real life—your dreams reflect your daily activities and thoughts. Correspondingly, nightmares are generally based on anxieties or tensions experienced during waking hours. It's no coincidence, then, that jobs are among the most common sleep-scenario subjects in the western world. Jobs and relationships. Jobs and relationships and being marooned on a desert island with Harrison Ford . . .

Um, where were we? Oh yeah, dreams. At any rate, if your slumber is regularly haunted by workplace phantoms, you're not as deeply troubled as you might think. Across America, employees are snuggled, all warm in their beds, while visions of guillotines dance in their heads. And since there's comfort in numbers, in our ongoing effort to keep you feeling well adjusted and entertained (not necessarily in that order), we collected a passel of these gruesome visions for your perusal. Along with Veronica Tonay, Ph.D., a psychologist who specializes in dream research at the University of California at Santa Cruz, we analyzed the living shit out of them. In the process, we discovered there are at least two levels of meaning for every dream: The external (how the dream relates to the objective world) and the internal (how it relates to your own personality and psyche). "As an adult, you often dream about your external world to act out internal conflicts," says Dr. Tonay. "All the characters in your dream—your boss, your colleagues—may actually be you. You're projecting aspects of your psyche onto others. So if you dream about an abusive boss, for example, on one level she really is your boss, but on a subconscious level she represents the abusive element of your own personality that you may fear or suppress."

Point taken. Submitted for your approval: A nine-to-five Night Gallery, carefully culled from the REM cycles of fitfully sleeping workers. We'll start with the four most common scary themes and then move on to some real humdingers. In reading these, maybe you'll learn something about yourself. Maybe you'll be able to exorcise a few of your own work demons. Maybe you'll uncover your subconscious hopes and dreams and evolve into a pillar of strength and virtue. Or not. As always, the choice is yours. Maestro, some Twilight Zone music, please. Without further ado, to coin what someone once said (we think it was Alice Cooper, but maybe it was Marianne Williamson): Welcome to your nightmare. Dee dee dee dee, dee dee dee dee, dee dee dee dee . . .

1. No Way Out

The Theme: I've Fallen and I Can't Get Up!

The Dream: "I'm being chased by someone, and I'm trying to escape, but it's like I'm underwater. My legs get heavier and clumsier, and my lungs hurt from the exertion. I'm frantic. I keep thinking: My legs won't work! I won't be able to get away! I will my body to move forward, but I'm veering and staggering. My chest starts to heave with sobs—what's happening to me? What's going on?"

1. "My boss is standing right in front of me, and he's going to kill me. I haul back to punch him, but my fist swings wildly and completely misses him. I keep trying and trying to hit him, but I miss every time. I have no

strength or coordination—my limbs feel like Jell-O. Finally, I crumple to the ground; when I look up, he's looming over me, laughing menacingly."

2. "There's an emergency, and I have to dial the phone in a hurry, but no matter what I do, I can't hit the right numbers. I keep hanging up and starting over; my heart is racing because I'm running out of time. My fingers feel like sausages, they keep jamming into the wrong buttons—eventually, I start smashing the phone with my fists, overcome by the frustration of it all."

The Scream: "Get me out of here!" The frustration dream is generally linked to a fear of ineptitude: You're faced with a task that's relatively simple, and yet you're completely incapacitated. And rather than working out a solution, you just keep going through the same motions—and failing. For the duration, you wonder, What's wrong with me? Why can't I do this thing that I should be able to do? According to Dr. Tonay, "You may be trying to run away from a potential failure—a stagnating job, a work conflict—but dreams won't let you do that. You need to confront in order to move on." What's more, you could be feeling trapped, unable to make a move (in the case of running) or a good connection (in the case of phone dialing).

The Scheme: Stop, think things through, and reassess. Identify what you think is your stumbling block and then determine whether your fear is actual or imagined. Do you really lack the skills to alphabetize the company files, or were you just bullied by the class spelling-bee champ as a child? If you honestly can't do the job, ask for help from a colleague or talk to your boss about redirecting your duties to an area where you feel more competent. But if your fears are unjustified, do your best to face and erase them. You might even bolster your confidence with some sort of mantra ("easy as ABC, easy as ABC, easy as ABC . . ."). Doing a reality check may put your frustration on hold. Using your speed dial's not a bad idea, either.

2. Strip Searches

The Theme: I'm in public and I can't get dressed!

The Dream: "We're in the middle of this big meeting, and suddenly, I discover I have no clothes on. There's nothing I can do about it; tentacles of horror slowly creep up my spine as I realize I have to spend the next few hours stark naked in front of everyone. I wonder how my body looks. I try to sit up straight and hold my stomach in, but I know it won't make a difference. I close my eyes and try as hard as I can to keep from crying."

1. "I'm going to a business lunch with a group of clients, when I look down and see that I'm barefoot. I think, 'Oh my god, I forgot to put on shoes this morning—how could I be such an idiot?' I wonder if anyone's noticed yet, and, if they have, whether I'll get in trouble."

2. "In the middle of a presentation, I reach for a pen in my skirt pocket—and I'm not wearing a skirt! I think, I can't believe this, I could've *sworn* I was wearing a skirt before. I'm now naked from the waist down. For a while, this seems to be totally acceptable, but then, all of a sudden, it isn't. People are whispering and pointing. I cover myself with my hands and try to run out of the room, but the doors are blocked by chairs. The

whispers swell into a deafening buzz. The whole room reverberates with the awful sound, while I just stand there, my arms at my sides, humiliated."

The Scream: "I'm vulnerable!" And how. Being caught with your pants down—or off—is one of the most common subjects of work-related anxiety dreams (it's also a prevalent dream among first-year college students). "Usually, the dreamer is uncertain of her personal or social role," says Dr. Tonay. "She's often going through a period of transition—maybe she has a new job, or she's questioning her work identity. She feels naked to the world, as though people can see right through her. She may be afraid that she'll be ashamed, hurt, assaulted, or exposed as a fraud." Or else, she's just not into shopping.

The Scheme: If you're spending nights in the Naked City, try to carve out a niche for yourself at the office. Familiarize yourself with the surroundings. Take your workmates to lunch, ask questions, suss out the office culture. Don't be a stranger, make yourself comfortable—odds are, they feel just as vulnerable as you do. Besides, you won't have to worry about being frisked if you expose yourself first. Another option: Go to bed fully dressed.

3. Test Patterns

The Theme: I'm being tested, and I can't get prepared!
The Dream: "Someone runs into my office and shouts, 'It's time for your presentation, right now!' My heart jumps—I thought it was due next month, and I haven't done a stitch of research. The person waves the deadline memo in my face—my eyes nervously scan

the page and sure enough, next to my name, there's to-day's date! My brain begins to pound. I feverishly start gathering papers, trying to think: Can I wing this? What will I say? How could I have let this happen?"

1. "The office is putting on a play for the CEO. We've been practicing for months. I have the lead part. We're all waiting backstage for the curtain to go up, when it dawns on me that I've missed all the rehearsals—I must've skipped them or something. I don't know my lines, I don't know my cues to go on, *nothing*. I grab a script and nervously thumb through it, hoping the lines will jog my memory, but it's no use. There's a huge au-dience, and someone pushes me onto the stage. The lights are blinding. I can't breathe."

2. "My boss calls me into her office and tells me I have to take a math test (in real life, I was an English major, and I have math phobia). I can't do it. I'm gripped with fear. I keep asking, How does this relate to my job, what relevance does this have? My boss barks, 'It doesn't matter, you just have to do this. *Now*.'"

The Scream: "I'm not worthy!" Test dreams are grounded in our old friend, Mr. Fear of Failure. Subse-quently, extremely goal-oriented people and over-achievers are most susceptible to this bedtime story line. The dreamer thinks, "This is my one big chance to excel, and I'm totally clueless." She might blame herself for negligence, or she might protest the unfairness of it all. "There are also some control issues going on," says Dr. Tonay. "Someone wants you to do the exact thing you're afraid of. Especially in the case of the math-test dream. The dreamer asks, 'Why do I have to take a math test when I'm clearly better equipped for other things? Why are you making me do this?' Possibly, she feels oppressed by undesirable duties—maybe she's sick of paying dues, for instance—and resents her boss for not allowing her to move up."

The Scheme: Don't shackle yourself with impossible expectations. This takes a certain amount of attitude adjustment. Remind yourself that you dictate your ambition; it shouldn't dictate you. Think "wanna" not "hafta." Squash your "inner stage mother" (to hell with piano lessons, you're going to the mall!). Life is not one big aptitude test, no one's keeping score. And ultimately, if you set reasonable goals, you'll meet with reasonable success. In the meantime, keep two sharpened, number two pencils on your night table—just in case.

4. Bodies in Motion

The Theme: I'm swamped, and I can't get a grip!
The Dream: "I'm the only person at our trading desk (I'm an assistant trader at an investment bank). Suddenly, the entire switchboard starts blinking like crazy—there are about a million calls coming in at once! I'm running up and down the length of the desk, trying to answer them all, and I can't. When I grab one phone, I disconnect another—and I keep losing all the messages I've written down. I'm scrambling back and forth, my head begins to spin, and I'm drenched in sweat."

1. "For some reason, I'm in charge of fifteen or twenty company cars, and I'm running through the streets, trying to find where I parked them all before they get towed. I'm clutching two fistfuls of keys, but

none of them are marked, so I don't know which key goes to what car. I wander around and around, putting different keys in different locks, and none of them fit. In the background, I can hear the tow truck coming—the more I frantically fumble, the louder it gets."

2. "I'm a beauty-products tester. In this recurring dream, I wake up surrounded by beauty products. I look under my pillow, and there's nail polish spilled all over. I open my closet, and shampoo and conditioner come spilling down on me. Powder and rouge are caked all over my clothes; there are giant mascara blotches on the walls and lipstick smeared all over everything. I'm completely agitated—where did all this stuff come from? How come nothing's in place? The situation gets worse, and I look around the room, filled with panic and distress."

The Scream: "Make it stop, make it all stop!" These sensory overloads are pretty straightforward. Sleep imitates life: You're deluged; everything's happening too fast, and there's no way to control it. "These dreams are fairly realistic," says Dr. Tonay. "They reflect the fact that you're feeling extremely stressed, and it's wearing you out." Maybe you have too many irons in the fire (as in the switchboard dream) or you're so inundated that you don't know where to begin (as in the car dream). Scenarios like the beauty-products blitz, Dr. Tonay says, "Might signify that the dreamer has a hard time separating herself from her work. She can't sort everything out—she keeps wondering why things aren't in place. She could have certain identity problems—cosmetics are a part of her job, but they may also symbolize that she's hiding her face from the world or struggling to create her own persona." (FYI:

The beauty-products tester happens to be an identical twin. Imagine.)

The Scheme: Slow down, get organized, and take a break. Focus on one project at a time; devise a system for yourself (e.g., a desk calendar, a bulletin board on the wall, a monthly schedule in your computer) that will minimize confusion. Try to decompress: Go for a walk, meditate, exercise, read a book, watch TV, have sex, avoid your mother. If you can't stand the heat, order take-out instead.

Don't mind if we do—we'll take two of the #4, and a half order of the #2—dressing on the side. That done, let's continue with our next set of night lines. In this portion of our program, the subject will tell her story, we'll toss out our analysis, Dr. Tonay will give her expert interpretation, and then we'll decide (with some help from the dreamer herself) whether we buy it or not. Yeah, that's right, we get the last word—you got a problem with that? What? Speak up. We can't hear you. Still can't hear you. You know why? *Because in Work Space, no one can hear you scream* . . . dee dee dee dee, dee dee dee dee, dee dee dee dee . . .

CAMILLE

Age: Thirty
Occupation: Executive producer of a national television talk show

I'm standing in a barracks, lined up with all the other employees in our division. My boss is walking up and down the lines, reviewing the troops. He has some sort of deputy by his side—no one I know, just this nameless, faceless guy. The whole place is completely, eerily silent, except for their two sets of footsteps, echoing through the building. As he gets closer, I realize his real purpose: *He's choosing who gets to live and who must die*. When he decides someone should die, he points to him, and his deputy puts a gun to that person's head and shoots him. Every few minutes or so, another single gunshot rings out and a person topples onto the floor. I'm frozen in terror, waiting for him to get to me.

The short take (from Val and El): Camille sees her boss as a murderous, ruthless person who has total control over her life.

The long take (from Dr. Tonay): The dreamer obviously views her work situation as a competitive place. It's common for especially driven people to dream about work in its most primitive state—for instance, they'll see themselves as soldiers or slaves. What seems clear is that a secret part of Camille would like to go in for the kill. When you have a faceless character in a dream, often that person symbolizes the dreamer. So here, the deputy is actually Camille herself—she's the person who will murder her colleagues, in cold blood, to please and/or obey her superior. The fact that she's also standing among the troops shows she's conflicted between her role as a fellow worker and her ruthless desire to ascend. Perhaps in real life, she's already sabotaged or hurt a colleague in order to get ahead—"shot" them to secure her own rank, so to speak—and she feels guilty about this.

The final take: When presented with Dr. Tonay's analysis, Camille admitted that her dream might have occurred during a time of office restructuring. "I was setting standards for people who worked for me," she said, "and if they didn't meet them, they were out." What she didn't admit (but we found out anyway) was that she actually played a large role in firing one of these people. In light of this, even if, subconsciously, Camille didn't want to acknowledge the "murderous" side of herself, her dream betrayed her. The way it looks to us, on an external level, she fears and reviles her boss. But on an internal level, she harbors a killer instinct—and while she's uneasy with it, she's also prepared to use it.

DANA

Age: Twenty-seven
Occupation: Booking agent for celebrity lecturers

I'm walking with G. Gordon Liddy through his house in the suburbs of Maryland. He's giving me a tour— he's kind of showing it off. I'm thinking it's a nice house, but I'm not exactly sure what I'm doing there. We're in the living room, when out of nowhere, we hear explosions outside. Liddy jumps into action—he tells me to take cover and then runs outside. The door is ajar. I peek through it, and see Hindenburg-sized chunks of chocolate chip cookie dough plummeting to the ground.

The short take: Dana was reading Tom Clancy books and eating Tollhouse cookies too close to bedtime.

The long take: In dreams, houses are recognized as symbols of the dreamer's psyche. Dana says the house looks nice, but she doesn't know the purpose of her visit. This could mean she recognizes she has a well-ordered mind, but isn't quite certain what she's doing with it. G. Gordon Liddy is a power figure—Dana may yearn for celebrity status and clout (her job choice would indicate that she does). Next, they're in the living room—the place where she lives, the part of her psyche that looks at her life—and they hear explosions. The explosions are outside; she chooses to view conflicts from a distance and doesn't really want to be a part of them. Still, the door is ajar and she looks through it: This is good; it means that Dana is able to see beyond herself and into the outside world. As for the cookie-dough bombs, here we have giant missiles made of kiddie food. Maybe she subconsciously feels as though her childhood's blowing up. She's thinking, "What happened to the ideals I had when I was a kid? Am I losing my youth?" Perhaps she's worried that she's sold out and left her more creative, childlike side behind.

The final take: We suck. Upon presenting Dr. Tonay's theory to Dana, she agreed with it, in spades. She told us that in the past few months, she'd felt as though she'd grown up too fast and was spending her adult life pandering to fancy celebrities and their egos. As a kid, she always wanted to be a novelist, and recently, she'd been thinking of trying to write, but never had the time. Tell us about it.

KARLA

Age: Twenty-eight
Occupation: Incentive planner

I'm working on a spreadsheet at my computer. There's this certain row of numbers that are called midpoints, and after a while, I notice that they're starting to quiver a little. They begin to vibrate and hum, and then they come to life. It sounds silly, but they're really scary—they have spikes and daggers and pincers that are snapping open and shut. They peel off the screen and menacingly advance toward me—I realize in a flash that they're going to kill me. I start screaming, "The midpoints are going to kill me! They're going to kill me!" (I found out later that I was actually screaming this in my sleep—I was so hysterical, my boyfriend had to shake me awake.)

The short take: Karla has math phobia (that makes two in one chapter) and isn't particularly happy in her job. She should sell her dream rights to Disney.

The long take: This seems to be a dream where the dreamer is struggling to integrate two opposing internal desires: Perhaps her obligation to do numbers' work versus her desire to explore less linear, more artistic or romantic pursuits. It's interesting that the emphasis is on *mid*points—maybe she feels caught in the middle of her two conflicting sides. On the one hand, she may feel that she benefits from doing this sort of math work, but on the other hand, she could fear that it's going to hurt her, thwart her creative ideals. There's also a chance that she has a conflict within the office—for example, an office romance that she's afraid will endanger her career—and she's torn between her romantic and logical sides. It sounds as though she needs to pursue the analytical part of her mind and not rely so much on intuition; by doing this, she may be able to actualize her creative aspirations.

The final take: Dr. Tonay aims . . . she shoots . . . she scores! To our credit, Karla is not a big math fan, nor is she doing jigs about her job. More than this, however, she disclosed that she does feel creatively stifled by her job, prefers to lean on intuition over logic, and yes, folks, she's also having a serious love affair with a higher-up in her company. So there's not much left for us to say except we hope they're very happy together.

Whew. Don't worry—our long, national nightmare is nearly over. But since we can't violate the First Rule of Handbook (whatever we make you do, we have to do, too), we're going to throw two of our own dreamscapes onto the pile. Consider it our friendly way of assuring you that our psyches are just as twisted as yours. More or less.

VAL

I'm in the office one day and it dawns on me that my boss, Roz, is a witch. She's not wearing a tall, pointy hat or anything, but she's all in black. She's an urban witch. I look at her face, and it's etched with pure evil. Suddenly, she sweeps through the hallway and swoops up the stairwell. I run outside the building and see her standing on the roof, engulfed in flames, cackling and waving her arms. She's loving the conflagration.

The short take: Roz = Witch who makes our life a living hell. Surprise!

The long take: Witches are archetypal of depraved parts of the psyche that the dreamer is afraid to confront. They embody amorality, power, destruction—they hit on the deepest, darkest secrets you keep, even from yourself. For Val, the witch isn't Roz at all—she merely personifies the unexplored, dark side of Val herself. Since fire often represents emotions, there might be a destructive part of Val that wants to set things on fire—or, on a psychological level, that wants to ignite situations with high emotion. The witch is laughing: She has a sense of humor. She's moving toward and reaching the top. Maybe Val secretly hungers for power. At the end of the dream, the witch is engulfed in flames. Externally, this could simply be wishful thinking—Val would like to see Roz cremated. Internally, it may symbolize Val's lust for power, her burning desire to ascend.

The final take: Well, jeez. It's not nearly as fun to jump on the bandwagon when it relates directly to us. Although we're more comfortable with the short take,

Val *was* intrigued by the possibility of having a flame-shooting, maniacal, power-hungry side. After all, she *is* rather emotional, and she does like to play with matches. Not to mention that her wardrobe is almost entirely black and, Lord knows, she does have a darn good sense of humor. Oh, dear. Be afraid. Be very afraid.

ELLEN

Val and I are driving in a car, and people are shooting at us. For some reason, we have to leave the car and make a run for it. I know the terrain, but Val doesn't. She can't keep up—if we go on like this, we'll be killed. So I find a safe hiding place—but there's only room for one of us, and it has to be Val since she doesn't know where she's going. I tell her, "Stay here and you'll be okay." We say a rushed goodbye—even though we know splitting up is the smart thing to do, it's still hard. We make a code so we can find each other when the whole thing has blown over. Then, I take one last look at her, curled up under a step, and run like crazy up the hill.

The short take: Since Ellen had this dream shortly before she left The Unnamed Magazine, we saw this as a harbinger of her departure. In Val's mind, Ellen left Val behind to get trampled by Roz (hence, the hiding place under the step) and, after abandoning her in a cramped, uncomfortable position, skipped off into the horizon. Ellen sees it as a heroic attempt to save Val's life while risking her own. Yes, well—we do love ourselves, don't we?

The long take: Ellen and Val start off in an enclosed space where people are shooting at them—this could represent an office where they don't feel safe. On an external level, the dream might imply that Ellen has more experience—she knows the terrain—and is ready to move ahead, professionally, while Val isn't strong enough to do the same. Internally, however, Val may represent the stumbling part of Ellen that she needs to let go of in order to survive. So both of them are really polarized versions of Ellen. Throughout the dream, Ellen is scared, but certain that she has the ability to pull through, as long as she leaves the insecure part of her behind. She needs all her strength at this point and has to shed her weaknesses in order to succeed. So she leaves her weaker self behind—the side that allows itself to be stepped on—and flees. Her movement up the hill signifies that she's ready to challenge herself and is finally rising above the conflict.

The final take: To avoid a civil war, once again, we'll bow to the wisdom of Dr. Tonay.

And . . . that's a wrap. At this point, we'd love to tell you how to avoid nightmares altogether, but we can't. Because you can't. Like it or not, the dreams will come. Oh, yes. They will come. Still, if you can't beat 'em, learn from them. You never know: The dark side of night may shed some light on your day. With that in mind, we're going to catch a quick snooze (hey, we've been up the whole chapter—*we're tired*), while you come up with **Misery: Your Top Ten Questions**. Make them good, okay? Okay. Nighty-night. Don't let the workbugs bite.

6

Misery: Your Top Ten Questions

2:17 P.M. Meanwhile, back at the dream ranch . . . The bull is right on top of you! She snorts out two small puffs of smoke, and as you take a deep breath to screech with fright, she opens her monstrous mouth and emits a terrifying . . . rrring! Rrrring-a-ling! You recoil reflexively, then stop mid-squawk and scratch your head. Ring-a-ling? That doesn't sound right. The bull readjusts her fierce stance, flexes her savage jaws, and tries again: *Rrrring!* Even *she* looks a little perplexed now. You blink at each other for a moment, slightly peeved by this irregular turn of events. What's going on? You're in the middle of wholesale slaughter here! How are you supposed to concentrate with that infernal ringing noise? Why doesn't somebody just get up and answer the . . .

PHONE! Your eyes fly open; you scramble to your feet and dive toward the noise. Too late—whoever interrupted your impending gore-dom hung up before you could thank him. You collapse back in your chair, bleary and disoriented. Wow. You must've dozed off for a moment there. You struggle to reenter the waking world; your head feels as if it's stuffed with cotton rags. How long have you been sleeping, anyway? Is there anything left to drink? What time is it?

You started snoring about fifteen minutes ago, there's a Diet Coke on your desk, and it's time to start a new chapter, of course. Before you continue in this vein, however, we want to remind you: The title of this chapter is *Misery: Your Top Ten Questions*. We just answered three. Since you just woke up, we'll consider them bonus questions, but after this, the meter's running. So if you really want to ask where your shoes are (on the floor behind the garbage pail), go ahead. But don't you have some more troubling issues you'd rather explore?

We thought so. Troubling issues are part and parcel with the nine-to-five lifestyle. Numerous studies have confirmed the downer effect of work: According to the latest figures from the Federal Bureau of Labor Statistics, 35 percent of us are dissatisfied with our jobs, not including the 8 percent of us who are unemployed. And from our branch office in Walden Pond, Massachusetts, sociology expert Henry David Thoreau reports that a whopping 90 percent of humanity lead lives of quiet desperation. Nonetheless, because government statistics and depressed transcendentalist conjecture are, you know, a bit *iffy*, we conducted a little poll of our own.

That's where you—and forty-nine of your browbeaten counterparts—come in. Upon picking your brains, we discovered that a full 96 percent of you were fed up with the daily grind. To add insult to injury, 58 percent expressed intense vocational hatred. Evidently, misery loves inquiry: In the course of our interviews, you asked more job-despair questions than we could shake a stick at. Still, since we hate to deny you anything, we cleared some space for the ten most urgent ones. Are you ready? Good. Then show us what you've got.

1. How did this whole mess happen to me? There's an old saying: Things don't happen to people; people make things happen. So, to a certain extent, you constructed your own bed of nails—and now you're screwed. But before you hammer yourself over the head, keep in mind that this is harsher than it sounds. Assuming you're not a total slacker, your biggest crime was probably over-optimism. You had a Perfect Job fantasy that merely didn't transpose into reality. (Sh)it happens. The fact is, the road to Office Hell is paved with good intentions.

Truth be told, it's less important to figure out *how* this happened than to simply acknowledge *that* it happened and move on. According to our poll, there were three main motivators that prompted smart women to make foolish job choices. The first one: Bigger bucks. "I can never resist a salary hike," said a thirty-year-old video marketer. "Even if I'm not sure the job is right for me, all I can hear is the ka-ching of the cash register. The dollar signs in my eyes blind me to everything else." (Money is the root of all evil.) Pure avarice wasn't the only cash incentive. A number of our respondents were less money-hungry than just plain hungry. "I was down to my last fifty dollars," explained a twenty-four-year-old paralegal. "I'd been job hunting for months, and I was desperate. When an offer came in, I took it, no questions asked." (Beggars can't be choosers.)

What's the best way to handle the green monster? If you're so broke that you can't even pay a compliment, just say yes. "Even if it's the worst job on earth, once you're on the payroll, you'll sleep better," says Harvey Mackay, a career consultant in San Francisco and author of *Sharkproof*. "You'll have health benefits and a regular income. Get your foot in the door, and try to find something better in the company, or network with people at other companies. It's easier to play when you're already in the game." On the other hand, if you're simply upgrading your handcuffs from gold to platinum, think twice before you lock yourself in. Our favorite rule of sum: If a move only affects the second digit of your salary (you go from $32K to $36K, for instance), your love for the job should be greater than your love for money. If the first digit increases by one and the second digit remains the same ($32K to $42K), your emotional and financial happiness should be about equal. If, however, the first digit goes up two or more increments ($32K to $62K—as if), well, that's a lot of dough. You're looking at a whole lifestyle change. Assuming everything seems legit (i.e., you're not delivering mysterious "gifts" to the nice customs officer at the airport), shipping out might be worth your while. Just remember: All that glitters is not gold.

The second motivator: Sheer laziness. "I've always ended up taking lousy jobs because I hate shopping around," admitted a twenty-six-year-old sales manager. "I jump on the first bus that comes along because I don't want to interview any more than I have to." (Leave no stone unturned.)

And the third motivator was, for lack of a better word,

cockiness. "Even though I'd heard horror stories about my boss-to-be, I assumed I could handle her," said an advertising copywriter. "I figured even though she treated everyone else like dirt, I'd somehow be different. I thought, 'I'm a special case—when she sees how talented I am, she'll come around.' She didn't. " (The bigger they come, the harder they fall.) Essentially, we're looking at some classic cases of covetousness, sloth, and pride. For you deadly-sin fans out there, this means we're batting three for seven. Not to worry, though—it's still your ballgame, so don't psyche yourself out on account of a bad season or two. You should view a lousy job experience the way you would a cliché (what, did you think we were doing this for our health?): It's universal, not overly long, somewhat annoying, and although it does deliver a certain life lesson, it's not the be-all to end-all. Live and learn. In time, you'll be able to trade in your old saw for a new, better one.

2. Will I ever get it right? Definitely—if you're willing to put in the time. On the average, our respondents took about two and a half false swings before they really connected. For some, it was a question of locating the right career path. Ellen needed a year of investment banking to discover she didn't much care for high finance, at which point she promptly switched into the low-finance world of publishing. Val worked for two years as a researcher before she realized she'd rather write fiction than check facts. Look, even Aristostle Onassis had to resign himself to the fact that he wasn't cut out to be a telephone operator prior to becoming a shipping tycoon. Moral: Don't be discouraged if you dial a few wrong numbers before you find your true calling.

Even when you do find it, you might experience some

static, courtesy of those grandes dames of executive recruiting: Miss Representation and Miss Communication. "At my last interview," said a twenty-nine-year-old hospital administrator, "the personnel manager made a lot of empty promises. It turned out that the job I accepted was nothing like the job I ended up doing." According to Mackay, "Misrepresentation in hiring is common. They paint the job one way—in-house promotions, great titles, and bonuses—but the reality is nothing like their pretty picture. The only way to safeguard against this is to do your homework first." Ask current and former employees of the company if the work environment is user-friendly. Be a policy wonk: Get the scoop on reviews, raises, vacations, benefits, personal days, relocation procedures, maternity leaves, job sharing, the hours, your expense account, internal mobility, severance packages, savings plans—the whole enchilada. Request second or third interviews. Don't let Henderson in Personnel mediate your future; talk to an on-site authority. Spend a day in the office—if you see an ocean of long faces, you'll know not to take the dive. In the meantime, don't worry about coming off as persnickety. *Au contraire, petits chats:* This kind of investigative reporting makes you look smart and discerning. Ultimately, should you take the offer, your employers will respect you all the more.

Clarity is also key. "I went into the job thinking my duties would be mostly editorial," said a thirty-year-old managing editor at a trade magazine. "Granted, my boss had told me beforehand that I'd be in charge of budgeting, but I assumed this was just a side responsibility. Boy, was I wrong. I spent most of my time balancing the books—not at all what I had in mind." Everything's subject to interpretation: One woman's sushi might be another woman's tuna casserole. To avoid any gray areas, be sure to get your job description in black and white. Discuss specifics; swap your wide-angle camera for a zoom lens. In the end, God (as in "God, I'm glad I found out 'Head of Marketing' really means 'chief food-shopper and lunch-maker!' ") is in the details.

3. When can I stop paying dues? Quoth Harvey Mackay, "You learn in your twenties, and earn in your thirties." A nice, neat equation to be sure (and we do so love nice and neat), but one that excludes any late bloomers in the crowd. After all, if you switch careers when you're twenty-nine, you probably won't get a corner office for your next birthday present. Our guideline for kids of all ages: Generally, you should plan to pay your dues in two- to three-year installments. This might seem like an unreasonably long serfside delay, but try to be patient. "No one starts at the top," says Mackay. "You have to acquire the experience of the people above you in order to work your way up."

Obvious, but true. Yes, we know you didn't take honors calculus so you could add up someone else's expenses. No, we don't think your boss gives you nearly enough credit for writing all your memos in iambic pentameter. But hang in there—you have to get polished before you can shine. Think in terms of early childhood development: When you were an infant, someone had to teach you how to walk and talk and go potty. You spent two or three years mastering these important skills, at which point you shed your diapers and toddled off to explore the great beyond. There was stuff to learn before you could play with the other kids; if you'd jumped straight from the womb into the world, you'd be crawling around to this day, covered with poop. Yeesh. Translated into adult terms, if you don't take the time to be properly trained, you'll land in deep shit. Wouldn't you rather log in hours at the Xerox machine now so that later on your boss won't pinch her nose and exclaim, "P. U.!" every time she sees you? Yes! Yes you would! Because you're a great big girl, yes you are!

4. I know I should look for another job, but I can't seem to get started. How come? Usually by manual stimulation—you? Before we get sidetracked by pleasure, though, let's stick to business. Job-search paralysis was prevalent among all the women we talked to. What caused their sit-ins? Oh, the usual gang of neurotic suspects, starting with self-blame. "Even though I knew my boss was a nut, every time she screamed at me, I felt guilty," said a twenty-six-year-old publicist. "I thought, 'If I can't do this job right, there's no way I'll be able to get another.' The longer I stayed, the more I was abused. And the more I was abused, the more I became convinced that I was completely unmarketable." In tough times, it's easier to blame yourself than to help yourself, but taking the easy way won't break those chains.

Other women were immobilized by their compulsion to make nice. "I didn't want to leave bad feelings behind," said a thirty-one-year-old retailer. "I hated my boss—and I'm sure the feeling was mutual. But even more, I hated the idea of departing on a sour note. I stuck around, trying to fix things so I could move on with a clear conscience." Granted, it's preferable to exit on friendly terms, but sometimes that just isn't feasible. You don't want to burn a bridge, but you don't want to burn an entire lifetime practicing fire prevention, either (future firefighters of the world, ignore that last statement. We think you're doing a great job!). Emotional neatniks should limit themselves to four months of fence-mending—beyond that, repairs are probably fruitless. Better to wash your hands clean of the whole unpleasant situation and get a fresh start.

Topping the list of un-motivators: Fear. "My job was utter misery, but at least it was familiar misery," said a twenty-four-year-old administrative assistant. "As awful as it was, I could predict the horror. Getting another job would've meant venturing into the unknown, which terrified me doubly. Besides, I was afraid if I started looking around, my boss would find out—and then I'd really be screwed to the wall." Often, fear manifested itself in the form of avoidance. In the case of a twenty-eight-year-old telemarketer, "Although the work sucked, the environment was pretty comfortable. I liked my office and had a few good friends—it seemed like too much trouble to make a change. Eventually, I was so lulled into complacency, I got agoraphobic. The unexplored job market became this scary, looming entity that I avoided at all costs." As someone once said (we think it was FDR, but maybe it was OB/GYN): There's nothing to fear but fear itself. And while we've discovered a number of isolated factors that disprove this theory (roaches, rodents, root canal, and other things that begin with "ro" like, say, Roz), it still holds plenty of water. The majority of our respondents admitted that once they took that first, excruciating step away from their "inner lackey," they felt more hopeful than fearful. Then again, don't take their word as gospel. See for yourself.

5. So in the meantime, how do I keep my hate from showing? Vigilantly. A hostile attitude stamps "Killjoy was here" all over the office like unsightly graffiti. "No boss likes having a negative presence on the team," says Mackay. "If you make your unhappiness known, you'll never stay employed. Hate is contagious—and everyone knows it. Keep in mind that there are ten happy, eager applicants who would love to take your place."

How very comforting. At any rate, as with all matters of artifice, some methods of faking are better than others. One twenty-seven-year-old investment banker tried to disguise her bile by smiling like a circus clown. "My intent was to send out positive vibes," she said, "but it didn't work very well. A colleague finally asked me why I was grinning insanely, and acting so edgy and manic in meetings. I didn't know how to answer, so I just smiled extra-hard—and started crying." Another woman decided to avoid personal interaction with her boss at all costs. "I communicated with her only through E-mail, voice-mail, and memos," she explained. "I thought I could fake happiness more easily if I never spoke to her in person. Big mistake: After a few months, she called me into her office and yelled at me for being a passive-aggressive wimp. Then she put me on probation." Yet another woman remembered, "Since I didn't have any acting abilities whatsoever, I tried wearing bright clothes to relay a sense of high energy. I thought if I wore yellow and orange outfits, my colleagues would assume I had a warm and sunny personality. All I ended up doing was calling attention to my misery. My boss could only look at my radioactive clothes for so long. Eventually, she had to look at my face, which was as grim and gray as November." A book editor said she tried to calm herself in the middle of the day by going to the museum; similarly, several women confessed to taking long gym breaks. Needless to say, going AWOL did not make their bosses' hearts grow fonder.

Mackay recommends a more Zen approach to disguising your vitriol: "Say to yourself, I can take any amount of pain, as long as I know it's going to end. Remind yourself that the pain won't go on forever, because you have the power to end it. You're the one in control." To make things more fun, pretend your office is an undercover work-recruiting base. They might think you're steadily toiling away for the common corporate good, but what you're really doing is heating up the phone and copier and laser printer to plot the next step of your brilliant career. (Maestro, some Spider-Man theme show music, please):

> *Job-Search Girl, Job-Search Girl,*
> *Watch her job-search plans unfurl!*
> *Spins her assets; quells her sighs;*
> *Catches interviews, just like flies—*
> *Look out! Here comes the Job-Search Girl!*

[Fade in to an office, where a figure sits at her desk, busily working. As the camera slowly pans in, it becomes clear that the figure is you.]

Voice-over: By day, she's a dutiful handmaiden, cleverly concealing her secret resentful identity. But beneath the disguise lies the fearless heart and shrewd mind of . . . Job-Search Girl! (A clock strikes five times.) Each night, she laughs triumphantly up her sleeve—

You (triumphantly): Ha HA!

Voice-over:—because, for yet another day, she has successfully fooled her villainous archenemy—The Boss. Little does anyone suspect that in a few short weeks,

Job-Search Girl will foil The Boss's dastardly attempts to destroy the hopes and dreams of America's youth, rescuing confidence and self-worth from the clutches of evil. And having completed her daring mission to restore justice and upward mobility for all (shot of you soaring out of your office window, looking unbelievably fabulous in a Lycra unitard with detachable cape, one fist outstretched in front of you) . . . POW! BLAMMO! KABOOM! She'll fly higher than ever before!

[Cut back to people milling around your office in confusion, as papers drift slowly back down onto a desk.]

Your boss (peering into the horizon): Who *was* that masked woman?

Oh, don't look at us that way. It's just a suggestion.

6. Great. But now that I've got all this bottled-up hate, how do I keep myself from exploding? Make like an air conditioner and vent. Find catharsis—strenuous aerobic activity and door-to-door charity work pop into mind (and then, oops, pop right back out). As a lower-impact alternative, exercise your jaw on a human sounding board. "Talk about your frustration to someone you trust," says Mackay. "Don't digress; keep the conversation to specific problems you have with your work, boss or colleagues. This is a productive way to identify conflicts, and sort them out." For the most part, respondents listed friends, lovers, parents, shrinks, siblings, coworkers, and that familiar face in the mirror as preferred confidantes. Several women also confessed to having passionate heart-to-hearts with their pets. "My little [cat] Starlight was the best listener," one woman gushed. "She always knew exactly how to cheer me up. We understood each other intimately." Golly. There's not much we can really add to that (except possibly: Cuckoo, cuckoo, cuckoo!). The point being, when you're feeling melancholy, a good dose of unconditional love can be a potent tonic.

If you want to confide in a coworker, fine—just keep a screen between your brain and your mouth. "Never discuss your salary, your sex life or health problems with people in your office," Mackay warns. (Of course, that doesn't mean you can't speculate on everyone else's salary, sex life, and health. A girl's gotta have some fun.) Moreover, choose your allies carefully. Never forget: The sympathetic face you're spilling your cake-hole to may have an evil flip side. "I made the mistake of commiserating with a woman who was also frustrated by the way our company never promoted from within," said a twenty-nine-year-old banker. "To improve her stock with our boss, she ratted me out and portrayed me as a real troublemaker. After that, my boss never trusted me." Even if you're convinced of your colleagues' loyalties, be sure to make your dissent sotto voce. "I was bitching with a group of people, and our supervisor overheard me," said a twenty-five-year-old business administrator. "There's was no taking it back. I was totally snagged." On a brighter note, one twenty-nine-year-old architect recounted, "I was going through a tough emotional time, and my work started piling up. I was afraid to go to my boss, so I confided in my office mate. When she saw what a wreck I was, she actually took some of my work and did it at home. She also gave me some constructive advice and got me back on schedule. She didn't do it for the glory because she never told a soul—she just sincerely wanted to help me out." So flickers a tiny beacon in the teeming darkness of the corporate world.

Finally, you could try tackling the problem head-on. This means when you have a problem with a coworker, you confront her and tell her how you're feeling. Or when you want a raise or promotion, you march into your boss's office and file your request. No trick lighting, stunt doubles, or fancy equipment—this is a bareknuckle one-on-one sport. And although some folks recommend the direct approach, we have to say we're a little apprehensive. See, when you're venting, or concocting elaborate revenge fantasies, you risk nothing. But by confronting your boss, you're gambling with sky-high stakes, and you'll either win or lose—big-time. "If your boss perceives you as a whiner or an instigator, she'll resent you," says Mackay. "And a boss who resents you is a boss who might terminate you." Boy. One of these days, that Harvey Mackay will have to come out of his shell and just say what he really means.

7. I'm in trouble at the office, and my colleagues are avoiding me. As if things weren't bad enough, now I'm the office pariah! How can I deal? Well, for starters, stop gnashing your teeth. Displaying row upon row of dangerous, gleaming incisors would scare off anyone—wait, did you say *pariah*? Ah. We thought you said *piranha*. Sorry.

[Val and El answer question #7—Take two.]

Well, for starters, stop gnashing your teeth; publicly obsessing over your coworkers' arctic behavior will only make you look like a victim. No, it isn't fair. Yes, they are big, fat, ugly stupid-head meanies. We don't blame you for feeling hurt, angry, ashamed, defensive, vengeful, crampy, slightly nauseated, and maybe a little bloated. And we wish we could offer a horse-sized painkiller, but barring Midol for the bloat, our doctor informs us that no miracle cure exists. Dr. Judith Sills, that is. She also says that approaching your coworkers with "Don't hate me because I'm hated" isn't a great idea because it'll only call greater attention to your ostracization. If you've bought it, don't flaunt it.

In the absence of a universal antidote, you might take the edge off by getting some perspective and attempting to depersonalize the situation. Tell yourself: It's not your paranoia, it's theirs. They're not so much hostile toward you as they are afraid for themselves (the yellow-bellied scum). This isn't rejection, it's protection. Bewail your fate on your own time—that's what friends and family are for. The next step, says Dr. Sills, is to "Recognize that, as unjust as your coworkers are being, you were in some way responsible for creating the situation. And if you have the courage to discover how you did this, you'll have valuable information for the future. To do this, pick someone in your office who you think is smart—someone objective and insightful enough to give you an accurate assessment. Go to her and say, 'Obviously, I've screwed up in some way. I've offended people, and put myself in a bad spot.' This will signal that you're taking responsibility. Then, tell her, 'I realize I've made a mistake, but I'm not completely clear on what it is. Would you be willing to clue me in?'" Choose carefully: You want a person who can go beyond "Gee, that memo you sent was weird" to "By distributing that memo yourself, you ignored the chain of command—and that's taboo around here. You've done this several times, and it's pissing people off." Not fun to hear, but "Imagine how useful this knowledge will be in later jobs," says Dr. Sills. "We make very few new mistakes in life; rather, we trip over the same bump over and over. You need to get someone to open your eyes to the bump. Because if you can bear having your eyes pried open, that's money in the bank."

8. Things are looking grim—how can I turn the situation around? In the words of Everyshrink: Why do you want turn the situation around? "You have to examine your motives," says Emily Koltnow, president of Women in Networking, a New York City consulting firm. "Do you want to make it work because you're afraid you can't get another job? Or because you're worried about not having a steady income? If security is your only incentive, don't waste your energy. Do yourself a favor and go elsewhere—channel your need for security into a job search instead." Then again, if you truly like the primary aspects of your job (the people, the company, the industry) and your problems are mostly secondary (the lousy benefits program, the 2 percent raises, the pig-dog who sits in the office next door), trying to turn the tide could be worth the effort. "Feeling happy in your field and really enjoying the day-to-day responsibilities are the best and strongest reasons for trying to keep your job," says Koltnow. "And when you're fighting to hang on, you need the most powerful motivation you can get."

9. Yeah, yeah, yeah. So is there any way to turn the situation around? Depends. The success rate hinges on two factors—timing and the nature of your conflict. The timing part is obvious: The early bird catches the stay of execution. "Smart workers are alert enough to nip potential job-ending issues in the bud," says Koltnow. Unfortunately, when it comes to office unpleasantries, most of us tend to make like Cleopatra and swim in denial. And we all know what happened to Cleopatra. As such, "Force yourself to monitor your performance from day one," Koltnow advises. "Be aware of how your boss responds to you and your work. And then, as troubles arise, try to solve them on the spot."

Assuming they're solvable, that is. This is where the nature-of-your-conflict factor comes into play. Office problems usually can be divided into two categories: Performance and Personality (bet you thought we were going to say Betty and Veronica, didn't you?). Basically, you're being rated on a first-grade report-card level; it's a "Sally works hard and demonstrates a fine knowl-edge of all subjects but has problems getting along with others" kind of thing. If the quality of your work is the issue, Koltnow suggests that you "Request a meeting with your boss. Say, 'I like this job so much, but there are certain tasks I feel I could be doing more efficiently. If you feel the same way, do you think we could discuss things and work out a plan together?' " This will indi-cate that you're aware of the problem and eager to fix it. Contrary to popular belief, most bosses don't like to watch their employees twist in the wind, so if you're not already too far afield, odds are, he or she will try to get you back on track. After that, it's up to you stay in the running.

Other work-related issues, alas, are beyond your con-trol. For instance, one twenty-six-year-old woman we spoke to worked at a small advertising agency where burning the midnight oil was *de rigueur*. "I wanted to take graduate courses at night, so I asked my manager if I could leave earlier on Mondays and Wednesdays," she remembers. "He replied, 'Everyone works late, and I can't give you special treatment.' The gist was: Keep up or get out." The options here are limited. "There's not much to do other than use any initiative you can," Koltnow says. "Keep tabs on why people stay so late—do you often have three meetings when one would suffice, or is there a way to speed up the flow of paperwork? Then, write up what you think would be a more efficient plan and give it to your boss." Present it as your personal effort to make *her* life easier and save the company money—no need to mention that you really just want to get home in time to catch the last fifteen minutes of "Baywatch." She might go for it, she might not—you won't know unless you try. On the other hand, if marathon hours aren't a matter of inefficiency (e.g., your boss's black hole of a social life means everyone has to hang out and keep her company), you're out of luck. "Either adjust to the schedule or find a more time-friendly job," says Koltnow. In other words, you can choose to simmer in the frying pan or take the fire.

But enough about work, let's talk about you—and how you interact with people at work. The upside of personality collisions, says Koltnow, is that "if you're willing to talk out the problem, and you're able to get to the heart of the matter, this kind of conflict can be the easiest to fix, partially because you're in control of changing your behavior." The downside is that they're so personal. And this makes them difficult to address in a clinical, businesslike manner (*you* try saying, "So, exactly why do you think I'm a major hose-beast?" without twitching just a little). Still, when you and your boss are clashing like two cymbals at a Tchaikovsky festival, your best bet is to face the music. "Ask your boss to define any problems she has with you," says Koltnow. "If the complaint can be remedied—for example, she thinks you have a negative attitude—tell her you'd like a chance to make amends. Schedule a review in a few months to determine if the situation is improving."

Granted, your boss's gripes may not be rational. Even so, you'll have to accommodate her tiniest, neurotic whim if you want to reverse the trend. "From the very beginning, my supervisor acted coolly towards me," a twenty-eight-year-old music marketing agent recalled. "No matter how ingratiating I was, she wouldn't bend. Then, a coworker clued me in: The umbrella I kept in the office had my previous employer's logo on it. Apparently, my boss had been fired by them years ago and seeing that umbrella next to my desk stirred up past resentments. I mean, how infantile can you get? Nonetheless, I got rid of it. I also made sure to comment in her presence how happy I was that I'd left my old company. In a few weeks, things were cozy as could be." Yes, it's absurd. But when you need brownie points, you've got to follow the recipe—nuts and all.

Friction among coworkers is another (horror) story. "Usually, this type of conflict is territorial," says Koltnow. "Someone thinks you're stepping on his or her turf. Rather than finding other allies, or being more political, you should confront your antagonist directly. This may be difficult, but it's the quickest solution. Sit down together and set clear boundaries. As a last resort, you might ask your manager to help establish some parameters. Defining your positions may lift the tension."

One last note: If at first you don't succeed, try, try— and then for god's sake, don't try again. Knowing when to pack it in can mean the difference between a good letter of reference and long-standing bitterness. Our suggested rotation period: Three months. After that, you'll only court moot. Which brings us back to that whole timing issue again. Isn't circular structure the best?

10. I'm at the end of my rope. Should I cut my losses and quit now or wait for the curtain to fall? If you've already been put on probation, then by all means, wait. You're only facing four more weeks, at the most—where's the fire? Whoops. Sorry. On the other hand, if you haven't been given a warning, you've got yourself quite a quandary. To facilitate the decision-making process, we propose this easy exercise: Lick your index finger. Place it at the bottom right-hand corner of page 139, and brush your hand in a swift sweeping motion to the left. Done correctly, this will whisk you straight to **Chapter Seven: Should I Stay or Should I Go?** But before you go anywhere, did you find your shoes? Uh-huh, behind the garbage pail—were we right or were we right? Okay, put them on, and grab that Diet Coke while you're at it. We've got a lot of ground to cover.

Dumb Boss Jokes

And we mean dumb. Then again, if you got off on serious, foo-foo intellectualizing, you'd be reading *The New Yorker* right now, not hobnobbing with us hoi polloi. Below, a dreadfully lowbrow array of cheap laughs. Hey, it's a dirty job—someone's got to joke about it.

What's the Difference?

Q: What's the difference between your boss and the subway?
A: Sometimes you miss the subway.

Q: What's the difference between a mosquito and a boss?
A: One's a relentless, pain-inflicting bloodsucker. The other's an insect.

Q: What's the difference between your boss and time?
A: You can kill time.

Q: What's the difference between your boss and a piranha?
A: Fins and scales. Or not.

Q: What's the difference between your boss and an artichoke?
A: The artichoke has a heart.

Q: What's the difference between your boss and a sperm?
A: The sperm has a one in a million chance of becoming human.

Common Laws

Q: What do your boss and Madonna have in common?
A: You never know who they'll fuck next.

Q: What do your boss and a tailor have in common?
A: They both hem you in, give you fits—and then you lose your shirt.

Q: Why is getting on your boss's bad side like having a yeast infection?
A: Either way, sooner or later, you know you'll get a discharge.

Q: Why is working in your office like having sex on the edge of the Grand Canyon?
A: They're both fucking close to death.

Q: What three football terms rhyme with boss?
A: Toss, loss . . . and punt.

Playing Favorites

Q: What's a boss's favorite vegetable?
A: Squash.

Q: What's a boss's favorite season?
A: Fall.

Q: What's a boss's favorite drug?
A: Crack.

Q: What's a boss's favorite soft drink?
A: Crush.

Q: What's a boss's favorite animal?
A: Cow.

Q: What's a boss's favorite hobby?
A: Crewel.

Q: What's a boss's favorite direction?
A: Right.

Q: What's a boss's favorite girl's name?
A: Barb.

Q: What's a boss's favorite boy's name?
A: Kurt.

Q: What's a boss's favorite color?
A: Gilt.

Q: What's a boss's favorite cereal?
A: Kix.

Q: What's a boss's favorite Broadway musical?
A: *Mame.*

Q: What's a boss's favorite car rental?
A: Hertz.

Q: What's a boss's favorite kind of lingerie?
A: Pink slips.

Q: What's a boss's favorite fabric softener?
A: Bounce.

Q: What's a boss's favorite dessert?
A: Turnovers.

Q: What's a boss's favorite store?
A: Saks.

Q: What's a boss's favorite sex position?
A: On top—and don't you forget it.

Say It Ain't So!

Q: What did the boss say to the cannon?
A: You're fired!

Q: What did the boss say to the ham?
A: You're canned!

Q: What did the boss say to the calendar?
A: Your days are numbered!

Q: What did the boss say to the baseball?
A: You're through!

Q: What did the boss say to Peggy Fleming?
A: You're on thin ice!

Q: What did the boss say to the bridge?
A: You're suspended!

Q: What did the boss say to George Washington?
A: You're history!

Close Calls

Q: What do you call five hundred bosses at the bottom of the sea?
A: A step in the right direction.

Q: What do you call a boss's term of office?
A: Acid reign.

Q: What do you call a smiling boss?
A: A figment of your imagination.

Q: What do you call an employee with two bosses?
A: A hostage.

Q: What do you call an angry boss?
A: Long-distance.

Q: What do you call a group of bosses around a fire?
A: Hell.

Q: What do you call an employee who blows her boss's brains out?
A: An excellent shot.

And Other Deep Thoughts . . .

Q: What does an assistant do with her asshole in the morning?
A: Brings him coffee and asks, "Do you need anything typed?"

Q: Why won't the mailman go to your boss's house?
A: Because her dog's mean, too.

Q: Why do bosses enjoy pillow fights?
A: They like shaking down.

Q: What's the best way to save a drowning boss?
A: Who gives a shit?

7

Should I Stay or Should I Go?

3:00 P.M. You're totally wide-awake now, fully focused, busy at your computer, playing Tetris. Despite that mother of a nightmare, you feel oddly revived by your nap. Somehow, in the haze between half sleep and full consciousness, you managed to resolve a bunch of work questions—like the top *ten* questions—that'd been gnawing away at you. Amazing. Who can begin to unravel the intricate workings of the human brain? Unfortunately, before the little "Nova" episode in your head can go any further, the phone trills. Fortunately, this time, you manage to answer it on the first ring. Unfortunately, it's your boss.

"And where, pray tell, have you been?" she snaps without so much as a howdy'do. "Here," you say meekly. "Oh, I think not," she retorts. "I tried to call you not one hour ago, and there was no answer. Obviously, you're too busy gallivanting to care about the

Rifkin project, so I'm thinking of handing it over to Stan. But since I'm nothing if not fair, I thought I'd give you a chance to submit three or four new account strategies before I make my final decision. Have them on my desk first thing in the morning. That would be nine A.M., by the way. I know you're a little fuzzy on when we start our day here." Click.

"Yes, well, thank you for that clarification," you say sarcastically into the dead receiver. "Many thanks indeed, you disgusting, oozing, pus-filled chancre. Do call again, you putrid, fat, flapping hole! Just tell the receptionist that *thy name is Lesion*!" Slam! Down goes the phone. Your chest is heaving; your hair is all sweaty. As the red mist clears from your field of vision, five words ring in your ears: *I . . . have . . . fucking . . . had it!*

You feverishly grab your pocketbook, sling it over your shoulder, and head for the door. As you reach for the doorknob, you suddenly realize you have no idea where you're going. Jesus! You make an angry about-face and start to pace the length of your office. What to do, what to do . . . You've put up and shut up for way too long (pace, pace); you're sick of being such a feeb (kick the desk, pace); you won't take this one sitting down, no sirree (turn, keep pacing); she'll be sorry because you're gonna, you're gonna (stop pacing, sudden epiphany) . . . *quit*. Yeah. That's right. You're gonna quit. You're gonna stride into her office and wave her hairy face goodbye. You'll say, "Later, Dog-breath—see you in the pound," and mosey on out before she even knows what hit her. Or you'll politely remark, "About the Rifkin account? I'm thinking you can just, oh, I don't know, eat me?" Then again, how about hitting her with the whole "Thy Name Is Lesion" speech? It doesn't matter; you'll decide when you get there. Time's a-wasting. The main thing is: You're outta here!

Whoa, Nellie. Not so fast. We sure do admire that fightin' spirit—but stifle it. This is a big step you're taking; no need to be hasty. Why don't you stop a moment to cool off—that's right, sit down and relax—and in a short while we can discuss things like reasonable adults.

Feeling better? There you go. Then let's have a little chat, shall we? Lean in close. A little closer. Can you hear us? Good, listen up: WHAT'S THE MATTER WITH YOU? ARE YOU TRYING TO KILL US? DID YOU ACTUALLY THINK YOU'D ACCOMPLISH ANYTHING BY STORMING AROUND LIKE A CRAZY PERSON, USING FILTHY LANGUAGE LIKE THAT? WHAT WERE YOU PLANNING ON DOING FOR MONEY? HOW ABOUT YOUR REPUTATION? DID YOU EVER STOP TO CONSIDER *OUR* FEELINGS? DOES OUR OPINION MEAN NOTHING TO YOU? *HOW WILL WE EXPLAIN THIS TO YOUR FATHER?*

Oh dear. So much for having a discussion like reasonable adults. Yes, we know, we've never even met your father. We lost our heads. But it was only because you were in such an overheated state (say, New Mexico); we got nervous that you'd do something rash and regret it later. And that would really stink. Take our word for it, we know from whence we speak. You see, years ago, one of us (we won't name names, but it wasn't Ellen) *did* do something rash. And she suffered for it. Oh, how she suffered. For six terrible months, she went through intense financial and psychological hardship, simply because, in a moment of snittiness, she foolishly uttered that fateful sentence:

Val: "You can't fire me—I quit!"
Ellen: No you didn't.

V: I absolutely did. Look, I was twenty-three years old, doing menial labor at a magazine. Eventually, performing grunt work made me deeply resentful—and I let everyone know it. I started to slack off; I made a few mistakes. One day, my boss walked me down the hall and said, "It's clear to us that you aren't happy here. We think you might be happier elsewhere. Your work isn't reliable anymore—I'm afraid we have to let you go." She said that I was entitled to a month of probation before they officially fired me. At which point, I blurted out . . .

E: Must you remind us again? I can't bear it.

V: Fine. I blurted out you-know-what, went back to my desk, put on my coat, and stalked out.

E: You rebel, you.

V: Not really, it was after five o'clock. The next morning, I typed up my resignation and distributed it to all the appropriate people. God, it felt good dropping those envelopes on their desks! I had this fantasy, see: I'd resign. They'd beg me to stay and offer me a promotion and a bundle of money. Fat chance. I got a few "good lucks" and "we'll miss you's," but that was it. I gave two weeks' notice, so for the next ten business days, I didn't do shred-one of work—I was a real brat. Not a smart move since the magazine world isn't big and a bad reputation travels fast. At the time, though, I only subscribed to the even smaller world inside my own head.

E: Small but colorful, Val. Small but colorful.

V: Thanks. Anyway, a few days after I decamped, a friend asked me why I didn't wait to get the boot. I said scornfully, "What, and give them the satisfaction of firing me?" Then she told me if I'd swallowed my pride, I could have gotten severance pay, plus $250 a week from unemployment. I was stunned. I had no idea. I felt like a . . .

E: Chump?

V: No thanks, I just ate. In any case, I made the classic mistake of thinking with my spleen instead of my brain. By not weighing my options carefully, I took it royally up the ass.

E: Gee, Val, any other body parts you want to mention before we wrap up here?

V: Not at this time, no.

Upshot: If you don't find out the whole truth, you pay the consequences. Now do you understand why we made such a fuss? We just didn't want you to get hurt. We hoped that (unlike us) you could learn from our mistakes.

Anyway, having unpacked our emotional baggage, we can explore the subject at hand with some degree of logic. Which is as it should be. Big career decisions like this require cool deliberation. Save the passion plays for your romantic life (see *The Heartbreak Handbook* for details); in the working world, impulse 'byes are rarely productive. Sure, vanishing in a cloud of angry smoke might seem like a dramatic way to fly. But when the dust settles, *you're* the one standing on the curb, with your coat in one hand, your cap in the other—and a pocket full of nothing.

Of course, this isn't to say you should *never* walk the walk. History is rife with accounts of great escapes. For example, the other day, we heard about a convict who broke out of his tenth-floor prison cell by climbing out the window (bear with us; we swear there's a point to this). Each day, this inmate was given a small piece of dental floss for hygiene purposes. Over the years, he saved about a zillion of these strands—*and braided them into a two-hundred-foot rope.* Pretty unbelievable, huh? Mind you, we'd never champion a crook on the lam, but we saw a metaphor in this story, and we couldn't resist. Would Mr. Roper have succeeded if he'd jumped out his window with only a half-baked scheme and a few inches of dental filament? We say nay. Rather, he had to gauge the height of the wall, assess his skills and resources, formulate a plan, and shrewdly implement it. And while we loudly condemn his criminal behavior, we've got to hand it to him in terms of strategic ingenuity. Lesson of the day: Think ahead. Also, always remember to floss.

So now that you've returned to a cooler state (say, Alaska), and you know the psychological requisites of a job exit (sanity, forethought), all you have to do is determine whether you want to sit or skedaddle. You'll need to consider a number of important factors: your financial status, professional reputation, threshold of pain, future career goals, immediate survival tactics, marketable skills, hopes and dreams, what your boyfriend's parents will think, if you should return the Ferragamo briefcase you just bought or keep it for interviews, how much longer we can drag out this list, and so on. One good step toward a final conclusion: seeking guidance (no, not the religious kind—everyone knows that God has been at the same job his entire life). After all, you practically conducted a nationwide poll on whether you could wear a taupe dress to a black-tie wedding—why not treat your career with the same magnitude? Solicit advice from people you respect or experts in your field. Many heads make lighter work of what can be an agonizing quandary.

Granted, the thought of all this canvassing is somewhat overwhelming. Not to worry: If you're too frazzled to go to the oracle, the oracle will come to you. To actuate this miracle, we assembled a panel of our most trusted advisers and posed the hypothetical question: Should I stay or should I go? And because homespun wisdom can often be as valuable as expert analysis, we queried a mix of respected authorities from both our professional and personal lives. Their answers provide compelling arguments for both courses of action. In the interest of fair play, we've alternated the pros with the cons (these aren't character judgments—we just mean the "stays" versus the "goes."). Ponder the evidence carefully before you make any conclusions. For our first witness, The People call:

Harvey Mackay: Never quit impulsively. You might have misread the signs—there's a chance that things aren't as bad as you think. Plus, corporate structure shifts all the time. In a matter of months, your situation could be completely different—maybe your boss will leave or your worst enemy will get transferred to another department. If you don't hang on for at least three months, you'll be making an emotional move, not a professional one. And when you think with your heart, you end up with heart disease.

On the other hand . . .

Rosemary Ellis, executive editor of *Working Woman*: If you hate your job such that it's cutting into your self-esteem or the quality of your performance, then it's time to go. Being chronically depressed in the office or doing sloppy work will only damage your reputation. Better to preserve your good name and get out.

Then again, on the third hand . . .

Val's mom: You just told me yesterday you were happy! What, could so much have changed in twenty-four hours? (Yelling to Val's dad) Howie? Howie! Valerie quit her job. My god. How will you pay rent? I guess you can move back home, but don't think for one minute that we plan to support you. I'm too upset to discuss this any-more—I'm handing the phone over to your father.

On the fourth hand . . .

Ellen Bravo, executive director of 9 to 5, The National Association for Working Women: Quitting is like moving. It's easier if you have a security deposit—money reserves or another job lined up. Have you maximized your power and minimized that of your boss? Did you do everything possible to fix the situation? Have you filed a complaint—even gone over your boss's head to complain? If you've tried everything and nothing works, your mental health is more important—and your only answer is leaving.

Of course, on the fifth hand . . .

Ellen's dad: Why don't you wait, dear? Just stay until you get another job—you know, it's easier to find a horse if you're already riding a horse. Or, you could always come home and live with us. We could eat lunch together, every day; nothing would make us happier. Think about it. Here's Mom.

Still, on the sixth hand . . .

A colleague of ours who didn't want to be named lest her comments besmirch her "fabulous" reputation: Definitely quit. Quit again. Keep quitting until they offer you more money. They will—at least they always have for me. Any time I've ever threatened to quit, my bosses have thrown huge amounts of money at my feet. It's almost pathetic, don't you think? What's that? It's never happened to you? Huh.

On the seventh hand, though . . .

Thomas Clawson, Ed.D., executive director of the

National Board for Certified Counselors: Before you do anything, seek counseling. This will help you figure out how to cope with the job, let you identify your strengths and weaknesses. Subsequently, you can focus your career path or find ways to enhance your skills. Be specific about your dislikes—by doing so, you'll be able to make a more informed choice the next time around. But until a contingency plan is in effect, I'd rather see an unhappy employee stick it out.

On the eighth hand . . .

Ellen's beloved: Go . . . go . . . go . . . Yes! Score! Did you say something, sweetie? Go! Yes! Can it wait until half time?

On the ninth hand, however . . .

Elizabeth Crow, editor-in-chief of *Mademoiselle* **and Val's boss:** If you're being fired for something that's not your fault—a personality conflict, for example, as opposed to a performance issue—let them do you the favor of giving you severance and unemployment. If the end isn't in sight, though, you need to get to the root of your discontent. Maybe you're not in the right line of work, in which case you should assess the measures you'll have to take to enter another venue. Many companies have tuition reimbursement programs: Take advantage of these programs and enroll in courses that will help you make a move. Should you plan on changing industries, stay employed—no one in a different field will want to hire you if they think you can't even hold down a job in your own field.

On the tenth hand . . .

A high-profile television producer (name withheld on request) who's had thirteen jobs, no firings: Life is too short to spend time being unhappy. I can't imagine that any career or financial goal is worth being miserable for. God knows, there's enough misery in other parts of your life—you don't need to have it at work, too. Often, personal turmoil can't be erased. But a bad job? *That's* something you can change.

Eleventh hand-wise . . .

Dr. Corey Goldstein, Ellen's dentist: Bite. (We assumed he was referring to biting the proverbial bullet, which would indicate that he recommends holding on to the job. Or perhaps he was making a broader comment on corporate society, as in "Work bites"? Tooth people are *so* inscrutable.)

And yet, on the twelfth hand . . .

Adele Scheele, author of *Skills for Success***:** If you're unhappy and you can handle it financially, go ahead and quit. Do it calmly and pleasantly: You shouldn't leave in a fit of rage. With a situation where you're angry, take a few days to become neutral. The world is too small and interdependent for you to sustain bad feelings about someone else (and vice versa). Furthermore, there's a chance that the only way you can keep things on friendly terms is by walking away.

Moving right along to the thirteenth hand . . .

Val's beloved: Leave your job? Didn't we agree that we'd both work so we could afford to buy a house? Plus, you said you wanted to keep your job until you were ready to have a baby! This is so typical! You're always saying one thing and then turning around and doing the exact opposi—wait a minute. Is this one of those hypothetical questions you're asking for your book? Jesus, Val. Why do you torture me like this?

On the fourteenth hand . . .

A personnel manager at a large publishing company: If the environment is crushing you emotionally, you should quit. You won't have the stamina to find something else until you're out of there. From a hiring stand-point, there's no shame in throwing in the towel. Just don't tell the interviewer that you quit because your ex-boss was a maniac—it won't make you look good. Manufacture a reason why you left—you wanted to free-lance, you were taking care of a family member, any-thing. This way, you won't seem random and unreliable.

But, on the—what is it, the fifteenth hand . . . ?

Helen Gurley Brown, editor-in-chief of *Cosmopolitan* and Ellen's boss: Even if your job is positively gruesome, I don't recommend quitting. The psycholog-ical impact of being unemployed can be enormous. I've had seventeen secretarial jobs, and I've been fired a few times. I remember once, when I went to pick up my fi-nal paycheck, I looked around the room and realized I was the only person there who wasn't working. I was the only one they didn't want. It was a terrible feeling. You probably won't be able to turn a bad situation around, so start networking on the job. Make calls during your lunch hour and actively search for other work. I know my employees have done this, and I never blamed them—they had to get on with their lives.

On the sixteenth hand . . .

Ellen's best friend at work: Fine. Leave. See if I care. (Bursts into tears.) You can't leave me, I'll die! Who'll I eat lunch with? This is horrible. I need a hug.

And on the seventeenth hand . . . we rested.

So there you have it: Our giant, sixteen-headed Oracle of Exits. For the record, Val urges you to do whatever Elizabeth Crow said; Ellen exhorts you to do what-ever Helen Gurley Brown said (we're no dummies). But as always, the choice is yours. What's more, be-fore you endorse any one recommendation, you have to determine how well it applies to your own particular state of affairs (say, Nevada). One woman's Velcro is another woman's Teflon. Consider the stories of Nancy and Candace, two women in the same line of work (advertising), whose careers took very different directions. Fortunately, both directions turned out to be right.

Nancy, twenty-seven: I'd been miserable for over a year. My boss fired all my friends during that time, and I knew she was hovering, waiting to swoop down and devour me, too. The pressure and anxiety became unbearable: In the fall I resolved to quit the first week of January. That way, I'd receive vacation pay and get my bonus. October and November were brutal. Then, on December 4, only weeks away from my planned resignation, my boss got fired. We were shocked—we'd always assumed she'd outlast everyone. The incoming boss turned out to be a godsend. She liked my work; she even liked me. Two years later, I've been promoted twice. It was worth the wait.

Candace, twenty-eight: My job was fairly enjoyable and lucrative for three years. Then, management changed—and I was faced with a whole different set of rules. From the outset, I sensed trouble, but my new boss gave me a raise and asked me to stay, so I did. Over the next few months, the whole system changed. I didn't feel like I fit in anywhere. Friends urged me to wait and get my land-legs, but I was convinced that this was futile. I didn't want to waste time. Against all recommendations (and much to my colleagues' surprise), I left. Two months later, the company went belly-up; the new owners drove it into the ground with all their "advanced" ideas. I was besieged with job offers. Apparently, other firms viewed my early departure as a savvy move. However inaccurate it might have been, this perception made me a desirable hire.

See? We do happy endings, every now and then. Okay, so far we've covered the importance of getting advice and how you should relate that advice to your own set of circumstances. Which leaves us with . . .

The Funny Quiz That Tells You If You Have a Quit, or Be-Fired Mind-Set

Answer true (T) or false (F):

SECTION ONE

1. At night, you have vivid fantasies that involve your boss, various sharp, carving instruments, and a freezer full of body parts.
2. During the day, you have vivid fantasies that involve the ledge of a forty-story building, a bunch of cute firemen, and a safety net.
3. When you hear your boss's voice in the hallway, you dive under your desk and repeatedly chant a Navajo curse that's said to ward off evil spirits.
4. Upon receiving an invitation to the big office Christmas party, you hurl it in your wastebasket and then dig it out so you can RSVP negatory.

If you answered True to three or more of the above, start getting your walking papers in order. Your behavior suggests you're not loud or obnoxious enough to get the boot—but not motivated enough to sit tight, either. Ideally, you'd seek and receive another job offer before you took off, but there's a strong likelihood you're too stir-crazy to defer to common sense. In any case, you have our vote for Most Likely to Pack

It In—and this makes you a bona fide Type Q (for further instruction, see below).

SECTION TWO

5. When your boss informs you that you're not getting a raise this year *(again)*, you thank her for her efforts and redouble yours.

6. After a colleague trashes you at a big meeting, you leave her a note apologizing for any conflict you might have caused when you protested that you actually were *not* a transvestite.

7. If a proposal comes back to you with an attached request to translate the entire thing into Sanskrit, you sign up for the next Berlitz course available.

8. Upon receiving an invitation to the big office Christmas party, you RSVP (Yes!) in person and offer to help out with the decorations.

If you answered True to any of the above, we can see why you hate your job: Playing the part of office doormat is no picnic. Nonetheless, you seem capable of handling a goodly amount of humiliation—and you strike us as being too prudent to give up your steady paycheck and bolt headlong into the unemployed world. So you might as well stay bolted (in place, that is) and use your free time to find work where the job description doesn't include pointless degradation. Incidentally, you qualify as a true-blue Type W (as in, Whatever you say, Boss)—details to follow.

SECTION THREE

9. When a memo about trimming down expenses circulates around the office, you take the department

out for a fancy, Frenchy lunch on your corporate card.

10. After your boss tells you that if you don't shape up, she'll ship you out, you salute and solemnly intone, "Aye-aye, Anchor-head."

11. At a meeting, when a coworker criticizes your work, you give her the finger.

12. Upon receiving an invitation to the big office Christmas party, you dash into the planning committee chairman's office, grab your crotch, and exclaim, "RSVP *this*, motherfucker!"

If you even think you could answer True to any of the above, don't move a muscle. Any day now, you'll be sacked. Consider yourself a Type T (for Take the money and run)—and keep reading.

If you're a Type Q: You'll have to follow a few standard eti-quit procedures prior to parting company. Start by giving your boss two weeks' notice. If there's a very good reason you can't do this (e.g., the transport pod leaves for your home planet in four days), talk to your personnel manager: She might be able to expedite the process. Otherwise, do the time—gladly and graciously. "You're still a paid employee for those last few weeks," says Juliette Miller, executive director of the National Career Development Association in Columbus, Ohio, "so you should act like one. If you don't stay conscientious all the way through, you'll hurt your reputation."

As for your resignation letter, keep it short and sweet. A litany of scathing indictments will only make you look like a sore loser—save them for your tell-all autobiography. Instead, try something along the lines of: *This is to confirm my resignation from the Exxon Corpo-*

ration as chief oil spiller on The Ides of March, 19XX. Sincerely, You. If there are any special conditions to your unemployment (e.g., paid health insurance, a company car), now's the time to put it in writing. Say *As per our understanding, Exxon will provide me medical coverage until my skin clears.* Sign your name at the bottom to make it official, and send copies to all the appropriate people, including the human resources department if you have one. You can voice your complaints at the exit interview—but don't go ballistic. You want your last impression to be professional, not confessional.

That done, get packing. Some firms will send your boxes home for you—find out what the policy is. You can take your Rolodex, personal files (that includes computer files on a disk), copies of any important projects you worked on, your stationery, a letter of recommendation (if possible), all your books and belongings, and your last pay stub (for tax purposes). You *cannot* take company-owned CD players, tape recorders, computer equipment, furniture, framed prints, cameras, and so on. Just because it's portable doesn't mean it's yours. Furthermore, ex post facto use of the corporate Federal Express and long-distance billing numbers is also a no-no. Contrary to popular belief, there's a good chance they *will* know the difference—so resist temptation. You might get away with taking paper clips, Post-it notes, a box of the rolling-ball ink pens you like so much, a few of those cool China Markers that peel 'round and 'round until they're completely naked, a big bunch of Jiffy pack envelopes, and gosh, you could sure use a good Scotch tape dispenser . . . You get the idea. Just don't say you got it from us.

If you're a Type W: You've got your work search cut out for you. Don't waste another minute: Type up your résumé, and make inquiries regarding possible job openings. While the prospect may be daunting, there's no cause for despair. For one, you've got a laser printer, Xerox machine, bond paper, and a great messenger service at your disposal. For another, says *Working Woman*'s Rosemary Ellis, "If an applicant is cast in a professional setting, she may seem more desirable. Because she's not sitting at home, waiting for the phone to ring, she won't appear desperate, although she very well may be."

A few things to remember while you're drumming up business: Keep up with your work, be as discreet as possible, and cover your tracks (i.e., don't leave incriminating information up on your computer screen, in the E-mail or voice-mail systems, or lying atop the garbage bin for everyone to see). Also, don't share job leads with office "friends." Call us cynical, but we've heard too many stories where Odette tells Odile about a great interview she has lined up—and two weeks later, Odette finds out that, by some strange coincidence, Odile got the job. Forewarned is forearmed. On that cheery note, happy hunting.

If you're a Type T: Go directly to **Chapter Eight. Playing with Fire** is a fast and furious game; if you don't have nerves of steel, you'll need to borrow them from someone, pronto. There's not much time, so brace yourself and hit the gas. We'll meet you there.

8

Playing with Fire

3:31 P.M. You're pumped. With a surge of adrenaline and rage, you lunge for the door, fling it open, and charge full-steam into . . . a person on the other side. Oof. As soon as your cheek hits the plastic pocket protector, you know it's Stan. The two of you let out little yelps of surprise, then regain your balance and warily step back. "I was about to knock," he explains. "So I see," you answer flatly.

You circle back to your desk and sit down, never taking your eyes off him. He awkwardly perches on the arm of a chair. "I want to talk to you about this morning," Stan begins uncomfortably. "I—I know you think I snitched on you, but I didn't. I mean, I did, but I didn't mean to. I mean, I *meant* to, but I couldn't help it. I mean . . . ," he trails off, flustered. "What's your point?" you ask, glaciers forming in your larynx. "My point is that Cujo called me into her office and asked me, point-blank, whether you were in yet," he blurts out with manic speed. "She caught me off-guard. I started to mutter some ridiculous story about a doctor's appointment, but then she fixed the Death Gaze on me. So I—I caved. I told her you weren't here. Now, she's making it look like I'm plotting against you, trying to steal that stupid Rifkin account. But I'm not! Honest to god! Meanwhile, Marnie and Joe practically called me Benedict Arnold to my face, and you, you're talking to me like you have glaciers in your larynx! I swear, I'm a pawn in her evil plot! I feel awful. I—I only wish you would believe me." His body sags, as if the effort of making this confession has dissolved some of his vertebrae. You look at the lines of tension forming parentheses around his mouth, the bruises of distress under his eyes, and you slowly realize: I know that face. That face is mine. It's mine and Marnie's and Joe's and everyone else's around here. It's the face that Cujo built. And just like that, the glaciers evaporate. "Forget it," you hear yourself saying gruffly to Stan. "We're all pawns. You had no choice." He smiles with wan gratitude. After a brief attempt to chat about nothing you'll ever remember, he shuffles out.

The rage is gone. You fold your arms on your desk and cradle your head in them. You think about Stan and his broken expression. Cujo used the two of you, like disposable razors. If you walk out now, you'll simply be another dull, discarded blade in her collection. As you ponder the bleak landscape of your future, a sudden revelation cuts through the thicket of gray: Instead of waiting passively to get shaved, why not stage a preemptive strike? Yeah, that's right—force her to push you out, cry foul, and make them pay for her error! A kernel of a plan sprouts in your brain. Grabbing a pen and paper, you write a single word, all in capitals, at the top of the page:

FIRESTARTER. Forget Drew Barrymore, this one's about you. For the first time all day, a wide grin spreads slowly across your face. Let the games begin.

And begin they will—right after we get a few things straight. Before rushing the field, please read and fill out the following application.

Yes or No?
- *Are you fully aware that you're staging your own termination?* Essentially, what you're doing is putting your hand on the ax handle and swinging it toward yourself—no ducking allowed.
- *Are you truly committed to this?* Because once you light the torch, there's no turning back. Win or lose, you're carrying that sucker all the way to the finish line.
- *Are you a mettle contender?* You'd better be made of stern stuff to charge the opposition. If you're afraid you might waffle or second-guess yourself at any time, put your fears—and plans—to rest.
- *Are you built for speed?* This round is sudden-death. If you're not financially and emotionally prepared to lose your job *in a matter of weeks*, stay on the bench.
- *Are you focused?* Forcing a firing takes complete concentration and organization. You'll have to get your act together—or take your show on the road.

All responses being yes, your mental faculties appear to be strong, which leaves us with just one more question:

- *Are you lying?*
Not to doubt your veracity, but in this arena, delusions are deadly. Self-ejection is a reality-based operation. Its success depends on your ability to collect

the facts and use them to your advantage. When you take on the corporate machine, it's your word against theirs, so you'd better be damn sure the proof is in the plotting. That said, let's review some of the more technical requirements. You're eligible to play if:

- You can establish that the job conflict is personal rather than work-related (e.g., there's friction between you and your boss, or you and a colleague who's above you in the corporate hierarchy).
- You can make a no-fault claim, arguing that circumstances beyond your control (illness, office conditions, your boss's little "diet-pill problem") are the source of your current predicament.
- Your manager alleges that your performance is substandard—and you can disprove her, beyond a reasonable doubt.

N.B.: If you fulfill the above requirements, *and* you belong to a religious, ethnic, or gender minority, you have an added advantage. It doesn't matter if your boss never showed a smidgen of prejudice: The very notion of a discrimination suit can bring even the hardest-nosed company negotiators to their knees. The beauty here is that you'll probably never even have to broach the topic of bias—they'll jump to that conclusion all by themselves. Of course, implementing this tactic is at your discretion; if you're uncomfortable exploiting your sex or cultural background, don't. Implying discrimination when none exists isn't exactly playing fair. Then again, have they really played fair with you? Call us cynical, but when push comes to shove, we say: Use it or lose it.

On the other hand, you're immediately disqualified from the tournament, if:

- Your unhappiness is based on the fact that you don't like doing what you're doing. In other words, if you get along with your boss fine, but you don't like answering phones for a living, it ain't gonna happen. Instead, try telling your boss about your frustrations—see if she can help you find another job, either internally or at an outside company.
- You work in an industry where getting fired translates to never getting hired again. While certain occupations (advertising, publishing, table dancing) have a high tolerance for job rotation, others (law, medicine, international espionage) do not. Assess how your actions will affect your future prospects.
- You already have a speckled past. A record of poor performance and bad attitude automatically takes you out of the running. Even if you succeed in getting yourself canned (probably not a difficult task), you might not be able to collect unemployment. Why? Because you were fired *with cause*.

Let's stop for a moment to clarify, shall we?

The Dreaded "With Cause" Clause

"With Cause" is an ugly little phrase that roughly translates to "She had it coming to her, the useless swine." It's your employer's special way of telling the government that your workplace contributions weren't worth a plugged nickel—and you should be compensated accordingly. The specifics of what constitutes "cause" vary from state to state (to find out your area's regulations, call your local branch of the Department of Labor). Generally, though, offenses that make the C-list include stealing from the office till, not doing your work or disrupting that of others (even after you've been given a warning), violating an established policy, tampering with official documents, or demonstrating clear intent to undermine your company.

Be advised that you can contest the charges. How it works: You get fired and apply for unemployment. The Unemployment Insurance (UI) office will contact your former employer to confirm the application. If they're informed you were fired with cause, you'll be denied payment—at which point you file an appeal. To do so, you'll need to produce a valid (typed, double-spaced) argument and written documentation that disproves your employer's claim (more on this later). A state-appointed administrative judge will hear your appeal; if he or she is unable to reach a verdict, it may be passed on to a committee of court-system judges. Again, the process differs slightly, depending on the state, but usually you have to plead your case in person.

Although this whole procedure sounds complicated, it's surprisingly efficient. You get ten to fifteen days to appeal—after that, you're out of luck. The judge will probably come to a decision within another week. And if you win, benefits will be paid retroactively.

Capische? This is why you must never blatantly act up in class. Get caught purposely trying to screw them over, and they'll return the favor. The whole idea here is to be fired by *mutual* consent. By dicking around, you'll destroy your credibility—and when you're finagling for a Section 8, credibility is crucial. Your word is leverage; leverage is your livelihood. Basically, you should consider your severance package as hush money. You wave something potentially scary in their faces; they pay you to stop waving. If you already have the reputation of class clown, you won't scare them a scrap. The class clown walks away with *zero*.

By now, it may have occurred to you that firestarting is a rough—and risky—endeavor. Consequently—

Val: Stop! Don't do it! Run away as fast as you can!

Ellen: Val. You're screaming. They're grown-ups—they can make their own decisions.

V: You're joking, right? I'm a grown-up, and I can't even decide between stripes and solids. My favorite designer is Betsy Ross. When I walk down the street, men in uniform salute me.

E: Are you done yet? You know, these self-deprecating riffs get you nowhere.

V: Spare me the lecture, okay? This isn't *The I Hate Myself Handbook*, you know.

E: Now there's a great book idea.

V: Too late, I think it's already been written. Didn't Roz model herself after it?

E: Other way around.

V: Ah. Which explains why, after two years of catering to Roz, you were inspired to act out your own little roman à clef: *The I Hate Working For People Who Hate Themselves and I Plan to Do Something About It Handbook*. If I recall correctly, it had a very riveting plot.

E: You flatter me. But really, I can't hog all the credit— Roz supplied me with much of the inspiration.

V: Could you give us some gory details, please?

E: I can try. As we discussed earlier, I'd been Roz's lick-spittle through a promotion and three raises, when finally her self-loathing spilled over onto me. We had that by now famous "I am so *not* freaked out" discussion, after which I realized I'd rather eat a cake made out of my own kidneys than absorb any more of her abuse. I wanted out—and I wanted them to pay my very expensive cab fare home. Since I had a lengthy record of good conduct and the conflict was personality-based—plus, I happen to be Asian—I was the perfect firestarter candidate.

V: If you do say so yourself.

E: I paid a visit to Patty, our personnel manager, and briefed her on the situation. I didn't purge my soul; I just lodged a few general complaints about Roz's unfounded antagonism. I also pointed out that I'd received a rave review, not six weeks before. I was careful to remain calm and friendly—I didn't want to alienate an important ally. Besides which, I really liked Patty. At the end of our conversation, she said something cheery, like "I really think we can turn this around." Puh-lease. Nonetheless, I replied sweetly, "I'm not sure it's up to me, but I'll do my best." I went back to my office, knowing that I'd dropped the first cordial hint of ill-tidings to come.

V: In other words, you primed the pump.

E: Exactly. That done, I started to assemble my springboard. I amassed a folder of all my work—story ideas, assignments, articles I wrote or edited, writers I recruited, memos I sent or received. I saved all written correspondence between Roz and me and made transcripts of every meeting and conversation we had. If Roz so much as blinked funny, I wrote it down. I was the best little paper-trail blazer this side of the Hudson.

V: If you do say so yourself.

E: My intent was to have proof of my diligence in the likely event that Roz castigated my performance. In the meantime, I completely stopped kissing ass. Naturally, the nasty memos and comments from Roz escalated. But whereas they used to upset me, now I welcomed them—each one was like another trophy for my freedom mantle. I watched my folder grow fatter and fatter, until—

V: The fat hit the fire.

E: Resoundingly. One Thursday night, I went to a party that was thrown by a former colleague. When I walked in, I discovered Roz had been invited, too. By then, relations were barely civil; she didn't even acknowledge my presence. Everyone at the party knew she was my boss, and the tension in the room was thicker than hemp. The very sight of Roz's cruel, flat face put me in a surly mood. I wanted to get her goat. So I did—I went over to her caprine boyfriend and started chatting with him. I flipped my hair. I touched his arm. After about fifteen minutes, I excused myself. The second I turned around, Roz's bony arm shot out of the crowd, yanked him away, and dragged him out of the party. Needless to say, she was livid; she was out of control—

V: She was so not *not* freaked out.

E: So *not* not. As she made her stormy exit, Roz seethed to a mutual friend, "Tien is going to pay for this"— proof again that her personal feelings governed her professional decisions. Sure enough, the next day she called my assistant and requested the honor of my presence Monday morning in her office.

V: Nice. You had the whole weekend to stress.

E: Tell me about it. On Monday, I sat myself down on her couch at the appointed hour. She said, "You're on four-week probation, starting today. I'll give you a memo detailing my problems with you later." I smiled sweetly, said "Great," and split. It was a very short prelude to the end of a very long haul.

V: So then what?

E: That day, I went over the situation with Patty. I said to her, "Roz is persecuting me for reasons unrelated to my performance. Although I'm unclear as to the *precise* motivation for her hostility, it's clearly personal. As you know, my file shows me to be a valued employee. In addition, I can provide documented proof of my work in the past five weeks, as well as records of all my interactions with Roz. Now, I realize when there's a personality conflict, the person of lesser authority is the one who has to leave—and I'm willing to do this. Quietly. But, in return, I expect to be generously compensated.

V: Holy cow. What genius wrote that speech?

E: My father. Dad instructed me every step of the way. He said the part about having "documented proof" would imply I was prepared for legal action. The part about being "unclear as to the precise motivation for her hostility" would jog the discrimination sector of their brain. The part about being "generously compensated" would communicate, Gimme, gimme, gimme. Evidently Father knew best because the message came across, loud and clear. Patty thought for a moment, then asked the obligatory, "Are you sure you don't want to try and make things work?" I said, "Patty, *really*. What would you do if you were me?"

V: Tough call since Patty had already witnessed six of Roz's other victims attempt—and fail—to make comebacks.

E: She was great. She looked me in the eye, nodded, and said, "Go do what you've got to do, kid." This was Monday afternoon. Tuesday morning, the company made me a severance offer; at the end of the day, I made a counter offer. On Wednesday, we negotiated further. By Thursday noon, we had closed the deal. I packed up my office, and on Friday at five P.M., I walked out of the building for the last time . . .

V: With a spring in your step and two more seasons of pay in your pocket. I've got to tell you, El, when you were haggling like that, you almost gave me a heart attack. I thought you were an idiot not to cash in immediately. But your tenacity paid off.

E: In terms of money, maybe. Emotionally speaking, those five days were among the most nerve-racking ones I've ever experienced. I felt like I was in a week-long high-speed car chase. It was a fight to the finish—and I sweated out every minute.

V: Well, it never showed. You were one tough cookie. You were the original cool customer.

E: If you do say so for me yourself.

And that concludes our first-person report from the inferno. Still interested in lighting up? Really? Stubborn little thing, aren't you? Well then, we won't even bother trying to talk you out of it. If you've got the nuts, we've got the bolts. Below, our own patented plan for fledgling firestarters. Or as we like to call it:

Twenty-eight Days to a More Fired You!

F minus four weeks and counting. Step one: Research your company's severance policy. Most established businesses offer one week to one month of severance for every year of service; all of them offer continued health insurance for a year to eighteen months (but you'll be required to pay the premiums—and they're not cheap). You're also entitled by law (whether you quit or get fired) to be paid for any vacation days you have left in the year. That's why people often quit after the first of the year—they automatically collect more vacation pay. All this information can be found in your employee benefits booklet (along with specifics on health insurance and pension plans). Get it. Study it. Knowledge is artillery.

If, for some reason, your company has no written policy, find out if an "understood" policy exists and what it is. In the rare cases where a company has no policy whatsoever, it's possible that severance won't be offered, no way, no how. You still need to get fired to collect unemployment though—so proceed.

Step two: Hit the paper trail. If you have a personality conflict with your supervisor, collect damning memos and correspondences; take minutes on any verbal exchanges; secure proof of your work efforts. Write down every abuse, every insult, every demand your boss hurls your way, be it coming in on weekends, cat-sitting, or requesting that you wear shorter skirts. Be neat and organized. This is the most important report you'll ever put together.

If you anticipate an ousting due to performance complaints, gather evidence that proves you're working as hard as you can. There's no shame in being a bad fit for a job, but there is in dropping the ball at this critical juncture. Keep a log of your hours (you'll be coming in early and leaving late, natch). Keep a list of phone calls you make in the office (they'll be work-related, of course). Keep records of every lunch and meeting you have (they'll be matters of official business, to be sure). Most of all, keep your nose to the grindstone. If your employer can prove your lack of productivity, you could get thwacked with a "with cause" charge. As we've established, that would be bad.

Make caution your watchword. You want to take them by surprise, so don't leave any plot clues lying around. Lock your folder in your desk every night; if necessary, take it home with you. Erase covert computer files after you've printed them out. Any electronic- or voice-mail messages that you want to add to your archives should be printed out or transcribed, then deleted. Nothing should be available for public scrutiny. This may sound paranoid, and it is. Do it anyway.

Finally, if the situation is undeniably abusive, you could call your Department of Labor. They'll direct you to the closest UI office. After you've been transferred twenty times and finally reach the right person, explain your position. Upon reviewing your complaints, they may grant you UI eligibility, in which case you can quit in comfort. And while this is a long shot, in worst-case scenarios, it's worth a try.

F minus 3 weeks. Open a dialogue with your personnel manager. Be friendly—after all, she's a person, too. Sure, she fires people for a living, but rent is rent. On top of which, you need her on your side. In the words of a Personnel insider, "If the employee is a jerk—even if her complaints are perfectly valid—I won't go the extra mile. But if she's a person I like and can empathize with, I'll do whatever possible to get her a good package. It's human nature—if she's nice, I'll be nice back." Listen and learn.

At that first conversation, be discreet. You're just checking in, so don't start unpacking—there's plenty of time for that later. Show up with a pen and paper and throughout the meeting take notes (this will make it clear you mean business, and you'll want them for your folder besides). Kick off with a simple "I feel my job isn't working out." Briefly list some reasons; offer a few concrete examples. At no time should you imply that you're interested in anything other than fixing the situation. As far as they're concerned, you love this job. If they suspect you're forcing a firing, your cover's blown. Toward the end of the meeting, ask the personnel manager to keep this discussion between the two of you: This way (a) your boss won't find out prematurely about your scheme and (b) you make the personnel liaison feel as though you trust her and consider her your confidante. With that one request, you're (a) covering your ass and (b) kissing hers.

You might also want to make an appointment with your boss. Choose a time when she's bordering on human (i.e., not minutes before a major meeting or before she's had her first cup of coffee). Follow the same general guidelines given above, but start by saying, "I've been with the company for X number of years, and it's become apparent in the past few months that our relationship [or 'my work,' whichever applies] is becoming a problem. You've indicated this to me in so many words [then give a specific example like "At last Tuesday's meeting, when I made a comment, you rolled your eyes, twirled your index finger around your temple, and muttered to the rest of the staff, 'What a nutjob' "]. I thought we might talk about how to improve matters." She may offer suggestions; she may not. The important thing is to get the ball rolling.

In these initial encounters, you'll be tempted to play your whole hand. Don't. It may be frustrating to hold back, but you'll need that ammunition down the road. Right now, you're merely establishing a few facts; don't cry or scream or start issuing threats. You're not in a position to make demands. Yet.

F minus 2 weeks. In addition to keeping your folder

up to date, you'll want to pay another visit to Percy Nell. The second time around, be a little more casual and confessional. This doesn't mean you should open with "Frankly, this stress has given me the worst gas! You?" Rather, stick with the job rap. Say, "To be honest, I don't sense that my boss thinks this is working out, either. I don't know what to do. Should we meet, the three of us, to discuss things?" That's right, you're proposing a conference à trois (we didn't say this was going to be fun). If Percy thinks this is a good idea, keep your mouth shut during the meeting. Let them do all the talking. Odds are, Percy will steer the discussion toward your boss's grievances. Since, obviously, your boss can't say she hates you because you have a boyfriend and she hasn't gotten laid in over a year, she'll have to focus on your poor performance. What she doesn't know is that you have scads of paperwork to counter her fraudulent claim. Keep that your little secret for the time being. Meanwhile, don't forget to take notes for your new best friend, Mr. Folder.

This is also the time for some reconnaissance work. Were you aware that most corporations are obliged by law to show employees their review files? We weren't. Request a private screening of yours. If you have a record of wonderful reviews, a promotion, or any raises, that's more fuel for your force-fire. Since you won't be allowed to take the file with you, ask to Xerox it. If your request is denied, get your hands on a camera, and photograph every page. Obtaining this information may cover your film-developing costs—and more.

F minus 1 week. This is it. You've assembled and Xeroxed all your evidence, you've lined up your sights, you've gone by the book—and now you're going to throw it at them. Hard.

Monday. Get an appointment with Percy, today. Try to schedule it for the afternoon (you'll be biting your nails all morning, but it's better to be able to leave the building immediately after your powwow). Bring an envelope containing duplicates of everything in Mr. Folder. Begin the meeting by saying, "Despite all my efforts, it's clear that—for some reason—my boss does not regard me [or my work] favorably. It is not *my* choice to leave, and I do not plan to resign. I have tried assiduously to repair the situation—*and the contents of this envelope will document my repeated attempts.* Nonetheless, my boss does not seem interested in a resolution. In light of this, if the *company* would prefer me to leave, I'm willing to discuss our options." The two key points in this speech: You're not quitting, and you want money. Be clear on this—leave no room for doubt.

If everything goes according to plan, Percy will probably ask for the envelope, please (make it known that you have the originals). Agree to speak on the phone the next morning, and return to your office. Your last task of the day: Compose a letter of reference for yourself. Be glowing. Print it out on company letterhead. Having your boss sign it will be part of your negotiations later in the week.

Tuesday. Your morning chat with Percy will reveal whether the company is willing to negotiate. She might ask if you have a severance figure in mind. Don't answer. Let them make the first offer; this way, you avoid getting lowballed. In theory, severance is not required by law, so your employee has every right to give you the brushoff. In practice, most companies will pony up at least a piddling amount. In any case, emphasize (nicely) that you'd like to have an offer before the close of business. Most likely, they'll be glad to oblige since they don't want to prolong the process any more than you do. When they make the offer, tell them you need to think about it. *You must never say yes right away.* Arrange to see Percy tomorrow, in person.

Wednesday. When you get to Percy's office, be ready to dicker. (Dicker? You hardly *know* her!) Say, "I don't mean to be difficult, but as it stands, I find this offer unacceptable. I'm sure we can find a reasonable way to amend it." Remind her of your years of dedicated service, your commendable record, your proof-positive envelope (not that she'll need reminding). Now is also the time to voice any thoughts—actual or implied—that you might have regarding discrimination. Next, outline what you consider to be an appropriate severance package. If your company has a written policy (which you've already memorized), use that as a framework for your requests. Remember: In the world of severance, everything's negotiable, so don't limit yourself to straight cash. If there's a ceiling on the number of paid workweeks they can offer, try to get additional weeks of vacation pay or wrangle for some bonus money. See if they'll cover your health insurance for a certain number of months or throw in company perks (e.g., car service privileges, use of an office and assistant elsewhere in the building, permission to keep your portable computer). Whip out your pretyped reference letter and request a signature. Settle on a "story" about your departure: Ensure that it won't be recorded in your file as a firing but as a "mutual agreement." Again, let them know you'll expect a response by the end of the day. If their second offer shows a 15 percent or more monetary increase, and they'll meet most of your other demands, ask for the specifics in writing. Tell them you'll give them an answer tomorrow.

Thursday. Go to Percy and graciously accept. Be grateful—tell her you couldn't have made it through without her (it never hurts to have a friend in Personnel). Make one final request: That tomorrow be your last day.

Cash in your outstanding expenses, and submit invoices for any unpaid commissions. Transfer all your personal computer files to a disk, and erase them from the system. Pack your stuff in boxes, and arrange to have them sent to you. Carry your Rolodex home yourself.

Friday. End of the line. You'll have to stop by Percy's office one last time to pick up your final check. Thank her again. Finish cleaning out your desk, and tie up loose ends. In the event that you have unfinished business with any people, inform them of your departure; if you can, tell them who your replacement will be. They'll appreciate your professionalism—and this is important since you might work with them again someday. Say your goodbyes, and exit whistling. Hold that head high, girl. Go home, go to a movie—Christ, go to Bali if you're so inclined. Celebrate. When you get a chance, call us up and tell us all about it (we can be reached at **Chapter Nine: Let Freedom Ring**). Until then, congratulations. You done good.

The First Thing I Did When I Walked Out of That Stinking Place . . .

- I told the security guards who escorted me out that I'd been fired because I found out my boss was a cross dresser. They believed me.
- I drank a vodka gimlet for each time my boss called me

an idiot. I'm not sure when I left the bar, but twelve hours later I woke up on my neighbor's couch.

- I ran into the field behind my house, flung my arms open, twirled around, and sang, "The HILLS are alive with the sound of music!"

- That night, I was going on a third date with this guy I really liked. He brought me a pack of Lucky Strike bubble gum cigarettes as a memento of my newfound freedom. I thought this was so cute, I broke my No-sex-until-the-sixth-date rule and slept with him that night.

- I went to see *Reality Bites* because it seemed appropriate.

- I walked over to the parking lot and did a cartwheel.

- I gave out the corporate Federal Express billing number to everyone I knew.

- My coworkers took me out to an expensive dinner—and charged it to the company.

- I got in bed with my cats and five paperback mysteries and didn't leave the apartment until I'd finished every one. It was bliss.

- I flew to visit my new boyfriend in San Francisco—and ended up staying for a year.

- I opened a giant bottle of champagne and toasted the night away with my roommate.

- Instead of looking for another job, I decided to freelance. When I got home after my last day, I found a box on my doorstep. My best friend had ordered me a cake; written in icing on top was the message: "Congratulations, Boss." Before I cut into it, I took a Polaroid—it's been sitting in a frame on my desk ever since.

- I had a terrible cold. As I was walking out, I blew my nose in a Kleenex and wiped it all over my boss's office door handle.

- On the way home, I passed the ASPCA and adopted a kitten. I figured I could use a friend during my unemployment. I loved her so much, I got another one six months later, even though I had found a job by then.
- I got in my car, put the top down, cranked the stereo, and drove like the wind.
- I went to my ex-boyfriend's house, took one look at him, and realized I didn't need him, either.

9

Let Freedom Ring

4:22 P.M. *Voilà!* With a triumphant flourish, you put the final touches on your Firestarter game plan. And now it's time to compile your folder of evidence. For once, your wastebasket phobia pays off: In every desk drawer, Pendaflexes bulge with papers bearing Cujo's pawprints. Oh, look, here's the lovely note she attached to your original Rifkin proposal: *FYI, In America, we spell it* judgment, *not* judgement. *Perhaps you should consider mastering English as a* third *language?* Apparently, Fraulein Rottweiler never learned that both versions are acceptable—but who cares? Either way, she's h-o-s-e-d. Next, a charming memo: *The simpletons in upper management will bore us with yet another ten-watt sales presentation, next Thursday at 9:30 A.M. Attendance is mandatory.* Simon says: Incriminate yourself! Oooh, here's a good one: *Due to this department's shockingly low productivity rate, no vacation days will be permitted between No-*

vember 15th and January 1st. As I shall be out of the office during the last two weeks of December, expense reports should be submitted to my assistant. Talk about pay dirt. With a cackle of glee, you rifle your fingers through the stack of indictments in front of you. This is great. This is so great. It's finally time for that dog to roll over.

As for you, the free world looms so close you can smell it, taste it, draw in long, deep breaths of it. Splendid, empty afternoons sprawl before you like a feather bed, inviting you to stretch out and linger in their poofy comfort. You will sleep the sleep of angels, feast the feast of kings, live the life of bliss . . . won't you? A tiny alarm sounds in your brain. How well do angels sleep, really, what with all that harp music? And don't kings usually feast on stringy wild game, like venison or pheasant or Camilla Parker Bowles? You're more of a Caesar salad girl yourself. But will you even be able to afford a bag of croutons on your scant budget? What if you end up sitting on the couch, steeped in jobless ignominy, eating frosting out of a can until your thighs extend over three different time zones? What if—? You feel your pulse pick up tempo like a high school marching band. Ba-da-dum. Ba-da-dum. Ba-da—NO. STOP. You give yourself a shake and sternly command your brain to shift back into Happy Gear. Think autonomy, not exile. Idyll, not idle. This is your dream come true. You've been praying for emancipation for as long as you can remember.

So now that it's almost here, why do you feel so pig-scared?

Bad news: You're human. (Good news: No need to worry about harp music.) The truth is, almost everyone has a love/hate relationship with unemployment. It's only natural. You cherish the concept of unlimited hours, but you dread the reality of limited funds. You can sleep as late as you want, but you don't have any reason to get out of bed. You're unfettered by the chains of corporate responsibility, but you're weighed down by the prospect of finding new, better chains. Let's face it: You could go on with this no pain/no gain list until the cows come home. *And* unpack. So why bother? As with most things in life, being in a jobless state (say, Arkansas) will always break down to equal parts good and bad. As such, the out-of-office experience depends solely on your perspective. It's a glass-half-empty, half-full kind of thing.

Being the ridiculous optimists that we are, we've chosen to focus on the full side of the glass. Considering that the average American adult spends one third of her life shackled to a desk, why not leap on this rare opportunity to run free? Granted, if you're the type of person who has to be on a payroll in order to feel truly alive, you should probably stop reading now. Because, to be honest, there aren't a lot of serious pavement-pounding tips here. The way we see it, droning, technical job-hunting stuff is for mainstream self-helpers, high school guidance counselors, and your Great-aunt Esther. We're more interested in feeling happy! And peppy! And bursting with love! And since we can't provide you all with round-trip air fare to Amsterdam, we figured the least we could do was not lay a heavy work-search trip on you. If this carefree approach to unemployment doesn't do it for you, we'll understand. But just so you know:

The Top Ten Job-Search Points
We Refuse to Make in This Here Chapter Are:

10. The most effective method of landing a job (success rate: 47 percent) is to apply directly to a person in the company of your choice, as opposed to going through personnel or a headhunter. Networking through friends, family, inside contacts, and your alma mater's career placement office is a close second (with a success rate of about 30 percent). By the way, employment agencies have a 5 percent success rate, so screw that noise.

9. The Help Wanted section of the newspaper is terrific—for part-time carnival work and "fabulous opportunities in entry-level telemarketing!" Makes you feel all tingly inside, doesn't it?

8. Résumés must be clean, clear, double-spaced, and fit on a single page. Work experience should be limited to the recent past. News flash: No one cares about the summer after high school when you were named "7-11 Employee of the Month" three times in a row.

7. The theory that every $10,000 you earn requires a month of job-searching is a fat load of hooey. What really factors in: the market, your skills, and your ability to market your skills.

6. The average job search takes anywhere from eight to twenty-four weeks. Dedicated work hounds spend at least twenty hours a week on the job scent (in their spare time, they make upside-down words on their calculators, join bird-watching clubs, and secretly read porn).

5. Small firms are better hiring bets than their megalithic counterparts. In the last twenty-five years, two out of every three jobs have been created by businesses of one hundred employees or fewer. It's not the size of the wave, it's the motion in the ocean.

4. One out of every five Americans is unemployed at some point during the year, so you shouldn't feel like a leper or anything.

3. At interviews don't feel obligated to answer any questions that make you feel uncomfortable (little tip: If at any time, your interviewer asks what your cup size is, you might want to rethink your career goals).

2. The interviewer doesn't have to do all the yapping. By coming prepared with your own set of questions, you look smarter and leave more informed. Try to watch your phrasing. Good question: "How does this fit in with your company policy?" Bad question: "What's for lunch?"

And the Number One Job-Search Point That We Blah, Blah, Blah in This Here Chapter Is:

1. Oh, we don't know. How about: If you grab the first offer that comes your way, you should keep this book handy for near-future reference? Or: Looking for a job is a full-time job in itself? Or maybe: It's your life, so only you know what works best for you? Whatever. Can you get back to us later? We just boarded the Peace (and Quiet) Train, three pages ago. Do you mind? *We're relaxing.*

Incidentally, we urge you to do the same. There'll be plenty of time to stress when your unemployment runs out (that would be anywhere from six to twelve months, depending on where you live). For now, why not allow yourself a set period of guilt-free frolic? Tell yourself, I swear I'll look for another job starting, say, February 30—but until then, I'll rest and recreate. Great-aunt Esther, be damned.

Besides which, contrary to popular belief, being unemployed does not necessarily translate to being unproductive. During Ellen's eleven-month period of joblessness, she wrote her first book and met the man who would later ask her to be his lawfully wedded housekeeper. During Val's seven-month hiatus, she wrote her first book and had a disastrous relationship that served as material for Ellen's first book. As it happens, writing and fighting are ideal unoccupational pastimes because they score high in two important sectors: They're cheap and they're satisfying. Nonetheless, math-minded pacifists can find plenty of diversion, too. If you know where to look, there's a wealth of cheap entertainment out there, tailor-made for the nonworking class. With this in mind, we rounded up fifty liberated women and asked them to share their secret pleasures. From their vast inventory, we picked out the top nine favorites (sorry, but one more list of ten, and we might have to hurt ourselves). Peruse them at your leisure. And should you decide to co-opt a few for yourself, by all means—feel free.

1. GET OUT. Across the board, we found that the first, joyful response to no work was all play. "I partied with old friends, new friends, strangers in bars, whomever," said a twenty-six-year-old ex-television producer. "I'd worked on a morning news program, so in my old life, I went to bed around nine P.M. and woke up at four-thirty A.M. I remember the first weeknight I was in a bar with friends when I realized it was after midnight—and the place was still *packed*. I thought, 'This is amazing. I'm actually going to have a normal social life.' " In the same vein, a twenty-five-year-old former photographer's assistant called her first few weeks of liberty "a giant game of catch-up. I'd been so busy working, I blew off a lot of my friends. This was my chance to make amends. I threw dinner parties—nothing fancy, just pasta and bread. I rounded up groups to go dancing or bar-hopping. I remembered birthdays and anniversaries—I compensated for all the times I'd been thoughtless in the past. I couldn't believe I let so many relationships slide for the sake of a dumb job. True friends are the most important treasures in the world." Aw. We'd brush away a tear, but our fingers are jammed down our throats. Scrape off the treacle coating, though, and we agree wholeheartedly.

The benefits: Having places to go and people to see will pleasantly confirm that there's more to life than billable hours. **The drawbacks:** Maybe *you* don't have to get up in the morning, but *they* do—and this can cause some conflict. "I used to get ticked off by everyone wanting to go home when I was still raring for action," said one woman. "They started avoiding me because I constantly pressured them to stay out 'just one more hour.' Luckily, I realized how annoying this was and put a lid on it." Another woman confessed, "When I was invited to friends' vacation houses, instead of going for just the weekend, I'd come in on Thursday and leave on Tuesday. By Sunday night, I sometimes sensed that I was overstaying my welcome, but I hung around anyway. I was in a selfish stage." Remember: Fun's fun, until someone gets pissed. **The consensus:** As someone once said (we think it was John Lennon, but maybe it was Yoko Ono), you get by with a little help from your friends. So now that you've got the time—live large.

2. GET OFF. In a surprising show of hands, 60 percent of our women confided that they started (or finished) their days off with a bang. In other words, they masturbated—some as often as thrice daily. "The best time to do it is right before noon," said a twenty-nine-year-old travel writer gone freelance. "You're home alone, it's quiet, and the phone usually doesn't ring. You can take a good half-hour to focus on yourself, free of outside interruptions. And not only does it feel good, it makes you hungry for lunch and gears you up for the rest of the afternoon." Some women used their "alone time" to bone up on technique. "I'd never really masturbated before," said a fashion retailer, once removed. "I'd tried, of course, but it was difficult to concentrate—I'd get distracted by thoughts about work, or roommates wandering around the apartment. When I lost my job, I suddenly had hours to myself—so I took advantage of this privacy and became intimately acquainted with my body. Now that I know my way around, my sex life's better, too."

The benefits: Increased heart rate, orgasm, peaceful meditation, a greater awareness of your sexuality, orgasm, a sense of physical and psychological release. Orgasm. Plus, you get your kicks for free (unless you use a battery-powered vibrator, in which case you're only out a few bucks a month). **The drawbacks:** Minimal. One woman felt that her habit detracted from her sex drive, which, in turn, detracted from her boyfriend's good humor. Another woman went at it with such enthusiasm, she put herself out of commission with a minor skin irritation. Yet another fell into the pattern of doing it once when she woke up, again at noon, and a third time around three P.M.—such that, when circumstances intervened, she suffered withdrawal. "There was a day," she recounted, "when I was dropping something off at my friend's parents' house, and I got stuck in a conversation with her mother. While she was gabbing away, I glanced at the clock and saw that it was three-fifteen. I started to sweat: I had to get home and masturbate! I cut her off midsentence, mumbled something about putting change in the parking meter, and ran out. I guess I was a little hooked." **The consensus:** With addictions like this, who needs detox? Go ahead. Have a ball.

3. **GET GOING.** Fifty percent of our respondents who were sloths in former lives found this the ideal time to launch a fitness regime. "I always *meant* to start running," said a twenty-eight-year-old ex–sales representative, "but I never got around to it. Once I wasn't in an office, though, I could schedule my day around exercising instead of the other way around. Anytime I felt like it, I could lace up and hit the road." For girls who joined gyms, unemployment provided the luxury of going at off-peak times, thus avoiding the rush-hour traffic. Moreover, our sweat set universally found that working out was good not only for the heart but for the head as well. "It gave me a feeling of accomplishment," said a thirty-year-old accountant-no-more. "If I did nothing other than go on a five-mile run or a long bike ride, I'd feel like the day was a success." Interestingly, the longer a woman was unemployed, the more likely she was to continue exercising after she found a job. "I couldn't find work for over six months," said a reformed slug, who took up aerobics after she got laid off. "By the time I did, my Jane Fonda tape had become a habit. I was so accustomed to doing it, I made a point of squeezing it in, no matter how busy my schedule was."
The benefits: Swimsuit shopping isn't nearly as trau-

matic as it used to be; plus, you feel virtuous as hell. Oh yeah, you're healthier, too. **The drawbacks:** You might overdo it. As one woman told us, "I was so psyched about getting rid of my flab, I became obsessed with keeping it off. I started working out three, four times a day. Fortunately, a sprained ankle forced me to cut back; when it healed, I kept to a more normal pace." As they say, all things in moderation. On another note, one respondent complained, "Buying new skimpy clothes really cut into my unemployment checks!" Bummer. **The consensus:** Just do it—within reason. Those bastards at Visa can wait.

4. GET THE STORY. After much coaxing, 45 percent of our off-duty crew confessed a weakness for daytime television. (Sure, they'll talk a blue streak about masturbation, but mention soap operas and they close up like bad clams. What's going on?) "I'd never watched soaps, but when I was fired, I got hooked on 'All My Children,' " said an erstwhile banker. "I watched it every day; if I had to be out for some reason, I taped it. I'd sit all alone in my house and shout things at the characters like 'Can't you see he's lying to you?' Or 'Erica, you moron—get a grip!' It was sort of embarrassing, but it was a release. I loved every minute." Many claimed that following a soap was a way of establishing continuity in their lives. "I didn't know where I was going professionally," said one respondent, "but I knew what the Quartermaines were up to on 'General Hospital.' In a weird way, having my own show was a stabilizing force." Other women watched, perchance to gloat. "No matter how bad things were for me, the characters in my soaps always had it way worse," said a former tax consultant, twenty-eight. "Watching them ruin their lives made me see that, in comparison, I was doing great."

The benefits: Catharsis, mindless diversion, an hour of escape from the real world, and the potential for some good big-hair laughs. **The drawbacks:** Like potato chips, sometimes it's impossible to have only one. Without realizing it, you've gone from eating lunch with Luke and Laura, to hanging out with Oprah, to having dinner with Pat and Vanna, to burning straight through prime time, until, before you can say "closed captioned for the thinking impaired," you're going to bed with Dave (Letterman, that is). **The consensus:** Stick to one a day, and you'll be fine.

5. GET HIGH. Scores, that is. Computer games were another big fix for over a third of our respondents. "I wouldn't even think of starting the day without a few hands of electronic bridge," one woman declared. "It was more important than coffee." Her fellow game-girls agreed in spades. The party favorites: Tetris and computer versions of Scrabble, solitaire, Parcheesi, chess, and blackjack. In the low-tech sector, many women did crossword puzzles, word searches, or cryptograms. Regardless of the game, all our players claimed that their chosen mind-sports improved their overall mind-sets. Said one wordsmith, "Playing electronic Scrabble was a way to keep my brain sharp. It was more mentally challenging than soaps, and just as absorbing." Another Tetris fanatic added, "Arranging the blocks in nice, neat lines and then clearing them away gave me a sense of order. When I stopped playing, I felt calm—it was like meditating." Game Boy. Don't get fired without it.

The benefits: Improved hand-eye coordination (for video gamers) and increased vocabulary skills (for Scrabble and crossword puzzlers). Also, as a Super Mario Brothers freak told us, "Every time I mastered a level and moved on to the next, I felt like I had accomplished something. Playing Nintendo was a way of setting personal records for myself. A small way, maybe—but when you're out of work, every little boost counts." **The drawbacks:** Again, you can get carried away. One woman told us how the Legend of Zelda nearly broke up her happy home. "My boyfriend would call during the day and say, 'What's going on?' I'd tell him, 'I'm out of the Light World and in a fairy cave. Can I call you back?' After a couple months, he finally proclaimed, 'It's the seven magic crystals or me!' I chose him. Reluctantly." **The consensus:** If you can limit yourself to, say, twenty, no thirty, no forty-five minutes a day, then go for it. You're entitled.

6. GET COMFY. Flying in the face of political correctness, 30 percent of our free birds chose to spend their off-hours nesting. Formerly nondomestic types suddenly developed an interest in throw pillows; women who were already thus inclined became even more so. "I'd always been a homebody," said a twenty-eight-year-old former bookkeeper, "but being in my living room all day, staring at curtains that didn't quite match the couch, threw me into overdrive. I made new curtains. I painted the bathroom. I dried my own flowers for potpourri. I guess my ugly work experience spurred me to pretty up my house." A former hospital administrator recalled how tidying became a form of therapy. "Instead of thinking about losing my job, I'd wax the floor," she explained. "If I was stressed about finding work, I'd clean the closets. When I started running out of money, I alphabetized my books—by author name, incidentally. Nesting was a great way to sweep away outside anxieties."

The benefits: You'll have yourself one fabulous

showcase of an apartment. Plus, during the Great American Cleanup, you'll find those sunglasses you—oops—accused your roommate of stealing. **The drawbacks:** You might become so fixated on home improvement, you forget there's life beyond your four walls. As our same hospital administrator said, "One day, it occurred to me that I hadn't walked out of my apartment in a week. I spent every day straightening, rearranging and scrubbing—I only stopped long enough to order in food. I looked around and realized my home looked as sanitized and orderly as the hospital I had just left. That's when I made a vow to get out at least once a day." **The consensus:** Unless you plan to pursue a career in interior design, try not to play musical chairs more than twice a week. Your life's already been turned upside-down—why add to the commotion?

7. **GET SPOILED.** For as long as we can remember, women's magazines have touted beauty treatments as the universal antidote. Feeling down? Have a manicure! Got the blues? Take a bubble bath! Whole family just got killed? Exfoliate! And while we hate to beat a dead beat, facts is facts: Twenty percent of our respondents loudly extolled the virtues of a good pamper-fest. "After working for five years with only one two-week vacation," said a twenty-seven-year-old off-duty attorney, "I was programmed to jump out of bed, shower, dress, and tear out the door in fifteen minutes. During my unemployment, I discovered the joys of not rushing. I took long showers, after which I moisturized every inch of my body. I waxed instead of shaving. I put hot-oil treatments in my hair. It was relaxing beyond belief. Taking the time to coddle myself helped me recuperate from all the years when my boss treated me terribly. As my skin

got smoother and softer, my confidence slowly returned." Full of self-hate? Moisturize!

The benefits: You look great. You feel great. Which must mean . . . you *are* great! **The drawbacks:** A bad tint job can ruin the whole month. Stick with cosmetic applications that leave no margin for error. **The consensus:** Yeah, yeah, yeah. Get your fucking manicure.

8. GET INVOLVED. Another 20 percent of our idle-makers undertook long-term projects to pass the time. The most common enterprises: making tapes, learning to cook, writing a screenplay or novel, gardening, painting, photography, and learning to play an instrument. Among the more unusual enterprises was the ant farm one woman started; another collected twenty-six rocks with the intention of painting a letter of the alphabet on each one (she stopped at P). And then there was the explosive little lass who tried to build her own bomb. "I wasn't going to use it or anything," she said. "I just wanted to see if I could do it." Righty-dighty. Despite the diversity, all these variations pretty much centered on the same theme: Structure and continuity. "I only wrote about fifty pages on my high school years," said one armchair novelist, "but it didn't matter. I really looked forward to working on it every day; it became my temporary raison d'être. Since I'd never written before, I felt a sense of creative satisfaction—something I didn't get from my job. I didn't intend to sell it or even have anyone else read it—I was just writing for me." Which is the best darn reason of all.

The benefits: As we said, structure and continuity. Weren't you paying attention? What's more, in one miraculous case, a woman's hobby actually turned into her livelihood. "I'd started collecting old Art Deco plates and cups from rummage sales. After about six months, I needed cash, so I took a few of my plates to a local overpriced antique shop. The owner loved them; she bought them for tons more than I originally spent. Now, I go to flea markets on consignment for a handful of stores and hunt for goodies—for a fee. I'm actually getting paid to do something I like." Showoff. **The drawbacks:** Not many. The ant-farm girl did relay a horrific tale that involved her cat knocking the formicary off a windowsill onto her boyfriend's mother's head and watching a cascade of a million teeming little . . . never mind. We'd rather not get into it. **The consensus:** Time and inclination are all you need to follow your dream, and since you've got both, reach for the sky! (We'd elaborate, but we're afraid we're—mmph, brff—going to be sick.)

9. GET CONNECTED. Finally, a passionate 5 percent of our women spent their off-hours getting on-line. For those user-unfriendly members in the audience, that's computer talk for when you hook your phone line into this little box called a modem, punch in a password, and then it somehow plugs you into the electronic-cyber-info-superhighway thingy that people are talking about these days (dammit, Jim, we're writers, not technocrats!). At any rate, you get to do all sorts of cool stuff like send electronic mail to your friends, or talk to other people who have the same weird tics that you do, or snoop around in various public files for trivia. It's like magic. If you have your own computer, jumping onto the Internet is certainly something to consider. A modem will run you about $100, and a subscription to an on-line "shell account" (e.g., America On-Line or CompuServe) will cost around $10 a month. There are also some full-access accounts available, but they're mainly for major computer geeks, so unless the shoe fits, skip it—you'll have to fork over way more money. What do you get for your investment? "An incredible range of entertainment," said a thirty-year-old stockbroker turned hacker. "I'd send E-mail to magazines commenting on articles. I'd talk to strangers all over the country. Sometimes, I'd pretend to be a man and talk to other men about sex. Other times, I'd pretend to be a journalist researching a story. I'd also log in a lot of comments about books and television shows." Deep.

The benefits: Where to begin, really? It's like a giant group computer game/rap session, but more so. **The drawbacks:** You can easily lose track of the time. "I'd start out trying to get some job-search leads," said a former graphic designer. "But then I'd sit at the computer and make cuter and cuter little icons for my display menu. After I settled on one, I'd have to tell all my on-line buddies what I'd done. Then I'd look up and it would be dark outside." (We're not exactly sure what she just said, but it sounds dangerous—so be careful.) **The consensus:** If all this strikes you as being more fun than you ever imagined, sign up for a month. It may be the beginning of a beautiful friendship . . .

. . . And the end of a beautiful chapter (not to brag, we just wanted to keep that parallel structure going). Anyway, now that we've hit a feel-good wave, rather than stopping, we thought we'd ride it all the way into **Chapter Ten: Sweet Revenge**. Join us, won't you? The last laugh's on us.

Love in the Aftermath

In theory, unemployment shouldn't affect your relationship one dot. After all, it's not as if you've suddenly become your evil twin (your grungy sweatpants-clad twin maybe, but evil twin, no). In reality, many a woman finds that once she gets her freedom, her boyfriend wants his, too. What gives? According to John Gray, Ph.D., author of *Men Are from Mars, Women Are from Venus*, the loss of a job can indeed alter the dynamic of a duo. Below, some of the most common rough patches that can crop up in love—when labor's lost.

He doesn't want to talk about your day——and at this point in your life, you need to talk more than ever. Let's face it: You're not exactly the paragon of security right now. Plus, after being alone all day, you feel like stretching out your vocal cords. The problem is, the minute he comes home/gets to your place, he heads for the couch, a beer in one hand, the remote control in the other. How to win his ear? Whining about how miserable and lonely you are will only make him turn up (the volume, that is), tune out, and drop off. Instead, Dr. Gray suggests, "To be polite, ask him about his day first. Then tell him about yours—but before you do, make it clear that he doesn't have to comment or give advice. You just need him to listen for a while. In fact, he doesn't even have to listen, he only has to *pretend* to listen." And after you've spewed forth for thirty minutes or so, you'll probably want to watch some TV yourself. Think of it as an episode of "Home Improvement" without the commercials.

You want to go out; he wants to order in. You're stir-crazy and ready to hit the town; meanwhile, he's beat and wants to hang. Frustrating, yes. But before you mash this potato, try to see things from his perspective. You've been singing the same old "C'mon, let's go out, we never go out, you're not any fun" song for weeks—why not hum a more productive tune? Instead of making vague requests (as in "I want to do something!"), get specific. Suggest a restaurant, look up movie times, call for reservations, buy the play tickets. He's been making decisions all day and doesn't want to make any more, but if you take care of the plans, odds are, he'll be glad to go along. And if he isn't, go without him. Rather than forcing the issue, "Tell him it's okay for him to stay home," advises Dr. Gray. "When you get back, rave about the food, the company, play up what a good time you had. Subtly relay the message that you don't need him to have fun. Once he sees it's okay to say no, he'll probably want to say yes." Fact: Men hate to feel they're missing out on anything. Why do you think they flip back and forth between channels all the time?

Now that you're not getting a paycheck, you're afraid he'll think you're a sponge. Good news: This may only be a concern in your own head. "He doesn't care if you're out of work or money," says Dr. Gray. "As long as you appreciate him, he'll be happy in the relationship." Is it really that simple? Apparently, yes. "Secretly," Dr. Gray adds, "he might even prefer it if you don't make tons of money. Deep down, a lot of men need to feel like the sole provider." Mmm . . . we have our doubts, but Dr. Gray *is* the expert. In which case, who are these guys, and how do we meet them?

He's annoyed because you call him ten times a day. This one smacks of the Him-not-wanting-to-talk-about-your-day problem. You're feeling listless and chatty, and you crave attention because your insecurity is high but your spirits are low, so you get kind of needy, and maybe a little whiny, but who can blame you since, gosh, you've got a lot of time on your hands, and so the least he can do is have a simple phone conversation with you, Christ almighty, is that too much to ask? Oh, dear. No wonder he's tempted to let his voice-mail answer. Better to call a friend, call a shrink, call the Coast Guard—if you keep pestering the poor boy, you might end up disconnecting him.

You're convinced he'll find you boring because you're unemployed. Again, Dr. Gray insists, "A man isn't attracted to a woman for what she does [note: unless she's doing it for him]. He wants her to like her job, but it's not the main attraction. If anything, he might be threatened by someone with a high-powered career." Maybe, maybe not. Then again, just because you're out of work doesn't mean you can't be your usual fascinating self. On the contrary: If you take this opportunity to go to new places, see new people, do new things, he'll see you as a refreshing break from the same old, same old.

Since you're not working, he expects you to cook, clean, and pick up his shirts. What's more, he's pissed when you don't. To which we say: Tough noogies. Just because you're in the house doesn't mean you're responsible for keeping it (unless you choose to). Granted, if he came home every day to find the house in total disarray, shades drawn, the remains of your lunch in the tub, and you in your bathrobe, sitting in front of the TV, picking your teeth and belching, we wouldn't blame him for being bummed. We do believe a little personal grooming is in order here—you know, clean hair can be a real picker-upper. In terms of home maintenance, though, you're not obliged to scrub for your love. You're his girl-friend, not his maid, so you can split the chores down the middle—just like you've always done (HA).

Let Freedom Sing

You've finally reached the sweet land of liberty, and it's time to celebrate. But what's a party without music? Here, our Top 40 (or so) list of high notes for the free world.

"Back in the High Life"—Steve Winwood

"Back in the Saddle"—Aerosmith

"Big Time"—Peter Gabriel

"Born Free"—Matt Monro

"Brand New Day"—Van Morrison

"Break My Stride"—Matthew Wilder

"Changes"—David Bowie

Chariots of Fire theme song

"Climb Ev'ry Mountain"—from The Sound of Music

"Don't Worry, Be Happy"—Bobby McFerrin

"Every Little Thing (is gonna be all right)"—Bob Marley

"Express Yourself"—Madonna

"Feelin' Groovy"—Simon and Garfunkel

"Footloose"—Kenny Loggins

"Free Falling"—Tom Petty

"Freedom"—George Michael

"Girls Just Wanna Have Fun"—Cyndi Lauper

"Glory Days"—Bruce Springsteen

"Have You Never Been Mellow"—Olivia Newton-John

"Here Comes the Sun"—The Beatles

"High Hopes"—Frank Sinatra

"Hit Me with Your Best Shot"—Pat Benatar

"I Am the Warrior"—Scandal

"I Can See Clearly"—Johnny Nash

"I Don't Wanna Work"—Todd Rundgren

"I Made It Through the Rain"—Barry Manilow

"I'm Free"—The Who

"I'm Still Standing"—Elton John

"It's the End of the World as We Know It"—REM

"Let It Grow"—Eric Clapton

"Let the River Run"—Carly Simon

"The Morning After"—Maureen McGovern

"Movin' Out"—Billy Joel

"My Life"—Billy Joel

"My Way"—Frank Sinatra

"On the Road Again"—Willie Nelson

"Pack Up Your Troubles"—Irving Berlin

"People Got to Be Free"—The Rascals

"Respect"—Aretha Franklin

Rocky theme song

"Salvation"—Elton John

"The Secret of Life"—James Taylor

"Strut"—Sheena Easton

"Sunshine"—Jonathan Edwards

"The Bitch Is Back"—Tina Turner

"The Impossible Dream"—from *Man of La Mancha*

The Mary Tyler Moore Show theme song

"The Tide Is High"—Blondie

"Tomorrow"—from *Annie*

"Walk of Life"—Dire Straits

"Walkin' on Sunshine"—Katrina and the Waves

"With a Little Luck"—Paul McCartney

And for a few visuals, try these on for size . . .

New Lease On Life

Baby Boom
A Christmas Carol
Doc Hollywood
The Fisher King
Joe Versus the Volcano
Night Shift
Regarding Henry
Splash
The Tall Guy
Trading Places

Against All Odds

Big
From the Hip
Gung Ho
The Lavender Hill Mob
Norma Rae
Rocky
The Secret of My Success
Tootsie
Work Is a 4-Letter Word

Now Who's the Boss?

Big Business
Big Business Girl

Business as Usual
How to Succeed in Business Without Really Trying
9 to 5
Secrets of a Secretary
Take This Job and Shove It
Working Girl

It Don't Get Much Worse Than This

After Hours
The Bonfire of the Vanities
The China Syndrome
Glengarry Glen Ross
Network
Philadelphia
Silkwood
Wall Street

10

Sweet Revenge

5:15 P.M. On second thought, maybe unemployment won't be so bad after all. You stare into space and visualize your life in the free world. Yup, there you are, all right, going to parties, buffing up your body, redecorating your apartment, writing a fabulous screenplay, accepting an Academy Awar—oh, whoops, that's not you, it's Jodie Foster. Never mind. In any case, at least your jitters have passed. With renewed determination, you do a final rundown of your Firestarter List of Duties. Morning appointment with Personnel? Check. Employee handbook? Check. Folder of evidence? Check. What does it spell? Cash.

Speaking of deposits, those two Diet Cokes you drank are threatening to defect. You were so preoccupied, the afternoon whizzed by without you doing likewise. Better skip to the loo. Quick like a bunny, you scamper down the hall, veer into your favorite first stall, and take a seat. Ahh.

Much better. You're in the middle of reading the PLEASE DO NOT FLUSH SANITARY NAPKINS sign on the wall for the eight hundredth time when the door to the bathroom swings open. Reflexively, you hang your head down to peek under the partition: A familiar pair of brown suede loafers shuffles past you and enters the last cubicle. "Marn?" you call out. "Is that you?" The rustle of toilet paper stops, midroll. "Yeah, but don't tell anyone," Marnie jokingly answers. "The boss'll dock my pay if she finds out I took a leak on company time." You both laugh—and stop abruptly as the door opens again. Clip, clop, clip, clop. A quick inspection reveals two black pumps parked in front of the sink. A red warning flag runs up your mental flagpole. Those cruel ankles, those intractable heels— they could only belong to one person: Cujo.

Great. The last thing you're up for is making bathroom small talk with that miserable sow. There are limits. The water runs for a while, then stops. What the hell is she doing? Through the buzz of the fluorescent lights, you hear a faint plinking noise. Aw, jeez. The woman is flossing! As you lean over for another floor-level scan, you see Marnie's upside-down face peeping out from beneath the divider. The two of you make eye contact; noiselessly, she mouths the words: *"We're trapped."* You roll your eyes wildly and mouth back emphatically, *"Tell me about it!"* Before this profound exchange can continue any further, a flurry of outside activity causes you to sit bolt upright. Abruptly, the black pumps spin around, click across the tile and out the door. Dog gone.

In unison, you and Marnie stand up, flush, and head for the faucets. You look at each other and then start to giggle uncontrollably; suddenly, being stuck in the bathroom is the funniest thing alive. "Our asses are falling asleep," you say between chuckles, "and meanwhile, she's flossing. Couldn't she just use . . . *Milk-Bones*?" Shrieks of laughter. Marnie doubles over against the wall, while you crouch by the paper towels. "Can you imagine if she'd decided to put on her makeup?" Marnie gasps out. "We'd be sitting on the can all night. The cleaning lady would've found us asleep, with our pantyhose bunched up around our knees!" The thought of this sends a fresh wave of hilarity over you. "Stop, stop," you protest, clutching your sides. "I'm crying, I can't . . . oh my god, I think I have to pee again." Yet another set of convulsions—you're afraid you might bust clean in half. Eventually, though, the hysteria subsides; You pull yourselves together and stagger down the hall. "See you tomorrow," Marnie says, ducking into her office. "It was a lousy day, but at least we got in a last laugh."

Boy, did you ever. Still smiling, you sit down, dab your eyes, and—wait a sec. An ugly thought seeps into your consciousness: Sure, you had a last laugh, but what about *the* last laugh? Just a dadburn minute. In the final tally, will Cujo herself be punished? No matter how much severance they give you, *she* won't sustain any personal injury. The money isn't coming out of *her* pocket. How could you overlook the fact that *she won't suffer one whit*! Unless—and now your brain starts to tick like a tiny bomb—you arrange otherwise. Doesn't one good turn of the knife deserve another? You've been down for the count long enough—isn't there one last score to settle? Tick, tick, tick, tick, tick . . . Before you can fully formulate an answer, Marnie pops her head in your doorway. "Haven't you left yet?" she asks. "What time is it?"

At that instant, you know. "It's payback time," you say.

So it's come to this, has it? After nine chapters of careful analysis and self-examination, you're going to jump pell-mell into a game of Follow the Spleen? Shoot your wad on a single, frenzied crime of passion? Let yourself be consumed by the howling forces of vindication? Cool.

Val: Cool? Are you nuts? We can't write *cool*! Our editors specifically asked us not to sanction irresponsible behavior. If they catch us calling revenge *cool*, there'll be all kinds of trouble. My god, just think about it. Professional disgrace! Legal bills! We'll lose the house!

Ellen: Val, relax. We don't have a house.

Val: Exactly! And why do you think that is? Because we keep strolling around, tossing out obscene words like *cool*!

E: Fine. Scratch cool. How about . . . red-hot? Is that better?

V (sputtering): Red-hot? Do you want to destroy us? Anything but red-hot! Red-hot makes revenge sound like the new trendy thing. What would ever possess you to use a terrible term like *red-hot*?

E: Gee, Val, I guess I forgot to tell you about that little bargaining session I had with Satan where he promised me handbook fame if I made extreme temperature references. It must have slipped my mind.

V: Very funny. I'm only trying to point out that we can't in good conscience condone grudge matches. We need to issue some sort of blanket warning, like: Retaliate at your own risk. Or score-settling can be hazardous to your career. Or—

E: Waiter, this soup is lukewarm?

V: Exactly.

Good. That done, let's get down to business—specifically, the business of revenge. No dinky storefront operation, this: Our research showed that corporate avengers were alive and well and punching clocks in offices everywhere. Amazingly, over half of the working wounded we interviewed confessed to recriminating pursuits. As an interesting footnote, office redress was generally deemed more socially acceptable than romantic retaliation. Apparently, a lost job rates as being more bruise-worthy than a lost love. Go figure.

Of course, just because other people are doing it doesn't necessarily mean you should. Like, if everyone were jumping off the Empire State Building, would you? Yeah, us, too. Even so, before you launch your counterattack, you need to consider a few things. First off: Lashback backlash (say *that* ten times fast). Since getting even is a key part of revenge (it's the whole middle part of the word, for Christ's sake), if you take a swipe at your boss, there's a chance she'll swipe back harder, and you'll swipe back again, until next thing you know, you're flying around in the *Enola Gay*, looking for an island to vaporize. Net result: Career falls down, goes boom. Look at the thirty-two-year-old woman who started out quietly by E-mailing a snide memo to her colleagues about their misogynist boss. He saw it on someone's computer and promptly made her the office spittoon (figuratively, that is). When she responded by "accidentally" spilling a cup of coffee on him, he dealt her a hefty pay cut. She countered by illegally releasing a computer virus into the company system, causing a megabyte meltdown. He called the police. Her final score: One pink slip, one arrest, one permanent criminal record. Crikey. The moral of all this being, not only can your initial potshot boomerang, it can escalate like gangbusters.

What's more, once you've taken your first hit, who's

to say you won't want another, then another? As one woman told us, "There was the immediate thrill of lashing out, but then it would fade, and I would start trying to come up with another prank to pull." Getting your licks in can be addicting: You experience your first high, and then you chase it—all the way to the Prozac factory. When you're in an emotionally heated state, it's just a few short steps from normal revenge fantasy, to sociopathy, to psychopathy, to a full-time job modeling straitjackets. Talk about giving yourself a hug.

Finally, all this scheming and conniving can be downright exhausting. The fact is, total indifference is probably more effective and less emotionally taxing. Then again, would you really want to slog through a whole chapter on total indifference? Yeah, us neither. Call us irresponsible, but in terms of reading matter, we'll choose prurience over prudence any day. As such, we decided to devote our final chapter to what someone once called (we think it was Aristotle, but maybe it was Bernard Goetz), the most wild sort of justice. Granted, a vendetta trail isn't a terribly rational route to take. But if you're dead set on bloodletting, neither sleet nor snow, nor all the rationale in the world will stay a revenge courier from her appointed rounds. Sometimes a girl's gotta do what a girl's gotta do. Besides, let's be honest: In that magic moment when your careful calculations come to fruition, revenge can be sweet. Cool, even. What can we say? Sue us.

Or better yet, join us as we take one last walk on the riled side. For your rubbernecking pleasure, we divided the following passion plays into five main acts: concealment, harassment, physical damage, humiliation, and professional sabotage. Oooh, we have chills already. So, if you've got the tits, get a load of these tats. In the meantime, remember: There's no such thing as a free punch.

Act One: Concealment

The method: You vent your aggressions by secretly doing naughty things that don't really hurt anyone. **The madness:** This has a very low risk factor—concealers usually commit petty infractions and rarely get caught. **The protagonist:** Someone who's pissed enough to move beyond mere revenge fantasy but passive-aggressive enough not to go bat-shit. **The staging:** Most concealers followed your basic "hide-the-bathroom-key" motif. Variations on this theme included hiding phone numbers, magazines, unfinished mystery novels, party invitations, remote controls for televisions or VCRs, cigarettes, ashtrays, and sodas from the office refrigerator. Additional covert maneuvers involved a monthly boss-roast, dartboards that bore the loathee's likeness, and spitting in cups of coffee. Oh, and we mustn't forget to mention that our own clever Val wrote a nationally published horror story titled "Roz: The Ugliest Woman in the World." **The players:**

- *Melissa, twenty-five, media planner.* Our boss was a major jerk who was roundly hated. The day of an important client lunch, one of my coworkers took a self-adhesive nametag that said, "Hello, my name is——," and filled the blank with ASSHOLE in big red letters. Then we paid the elevator guy ten bucks to secretly stick the sign on our supervisor's back as he was leaving for lunch. The best part was, when our boss got back, the tag was still there. No one had told him about it, and he wore it all day. It was great.

- *Leila, twenty-six, investment banker.* The head trader in our division was known for his terrible temper, which he regularly unleashed on me. He often walked around our desk in his stocking feet, so a half-hour before his annual performance review, I hid his shoes to get back at him. He freaked. He started running around screaming, "Where are my goddamn shoes? Who the hell took my shoes?" He made a huge scene in the middle of the trading floor, cursing and shouting over a pair of shoes. People's faces were twitching from trying not to laugh—mine most of all. Finally, someone lent him a new pair of sneakers, a size too large. He looked like such a major dork in his dark suit and big white Nikes—afterwards, even the managing director who reviewed him made jokes about it.

- *Carrie, twenty-six, catalogue proofreader.* I was working at a mail-order catalogue where the publisher spent her days screaming at us. No matter what we did, she'd find something to criticize. Ironically, her name was Pleasant. The entire staff finally banded together and wrote a romance novel entitled *Love Among the Layouts,* that took place in our office and ended with Pleasant's gruesome murder. Every departing employee got a personal copy.

- *Alma, twenty-two, executive assistant.* My boss treated me like a slave—she used to send me all over town for her lunch. I'd have to go to one place for her favorite sandwich, another place for her cappuccino, yet another for some special kind of dessert, and so on. This particular time, I'd spent about an hour in the pouring rain, running around to fill her various food orders. When I returned, there was a note from my boss: She was at a meeting upstairs in the CEO's office; I was to serve her lunch there. I unwrapped everything, arranged a tray, and carried it up two flights of stairs, like I was her personal waiter. The minute I got back to my desk, the phone rang. It was my boss—she wanted me to wash her pear for her. I was furious. I went back upstairs, took the pear, brought it to the bathroom—and something in me snapped. Holding the pear by its stem, I dunked it in a toilet. I ran it underneath the seat rim, sloshed it around—when I was finished, the toilet was virtually spotless. I brought the dripping wet pear back to my boss, who put it on a table. It started to roll off the edge, but she caught it and squealed, "Oh! My clean pear almost fell on the floor!" I thought, "Honey, hitting the carpet would be the best thing that could happen to that pear." As I was leaving, I looked over my shoulder and saw her take the first bite.

The rating: G, Generally harmless. Concealment is so penny ante, just about anyone can pull it off, unless they're total chickens (in which case: Balk, balk-balk, balk, balk!). **The curtain call:** Well, it depends. Like, when you watched *The Little Mermaid*, were you restless, mildly entertained, or deeply fulfilled? If small potatoes will take the edge off your hunger, you're in the right place.

Act Two: Harassment

The method: In a nutshell, pestering. You become an anonymous thorn in your boss's side. **The madness:**

Piddling to middling. Again, the degree of danger is low, as long as you don't get snagged. **The protagonist:** An employee whose thirst for blood is more on the level of a mosquito than a vampire. **The staging:** Crank calls topped the list here, followed by signing the enemy up for unwanted magazine subscriptions, record-club memberships, and fan clubs. Sending pizzas and limousines were also common, as were arranging cancellations of home electricity, telephone and cable service, and credit cards. **The players:**

- *Christine, twenty-six, art gallery assistant.* For a year, I assisted a gallery manager who second-guessed everything I did. I wanted her to know how it felt to be constantly besieged by stupid questions. So I made a bunch of signs that said, FOR SALE: MERCEDES 525 CONVERTIBLE, PRACTICALLY NEW, HAS ONLY BEEN DRIVEN 1100 MILES. ASKING $2500 OR BEST OFFER. MUST SELL. CALL ANY TIME, DAY OR NIGHT. I put her name and home phone number at the bottom of each notice and hung them up all over the city. She must have gotten a million calls—every day her answering-machine tape was filled to capacity. Four months later, prospective buyers were still calling. She was so stressed out, she didn't have the energy to hassle me nearly as much.

- *Ginny, twenty-five, paralegal.* I was assigned to an attorney who was a real nut case—I mean, the woman was certifiably insane. She made my life miserable. I began to send her plain, white postcards, one a week. On the first one, I wrote, *Lithium?* The next one read, *Halcion?*, the third, *Shock Treatment?*, and so on. With each additional card, the handwriting got shakier and weirder. On the tenth one, I wrote,

I know where you live, in the most psychotic scrawl imaginable. That's when she wigged out completely. She took a leave of absence and went to visit her sister who lived in Vienna. In her absence, I got transferred to a partner who was the perfect boss. At first, I felt kind of guilty—but I got over it.

- *Tina, twenty-nine, sales representative.* I'd been working at the same firm for about three years, when our department head retired. His replacement was Hitler reincarnate. One day, I was sitting in my office crying over yet another harsh thing he'd said, when I decided, *That's it.* I was racking my brains for a way to make him cry, when I remembered that he was wildly allergic to cats. That night, I brushed my cat and saved all the fur. The next morning, I woke up at dawn, snuck into his office, and covered everything with an imperceptible layer of cat hair. For good measure, I sprinkled some used cat litter in the nooks and crannies around his desk. I didn't ruin anything, I just *tainted* it. I repeated this every few days or so, for about three months. And although I'm not usually a mean person, I have to say I got intense satisfaction from listening to his desperate sneezing, seeing his watery eyes and bloated face. Plus, my cat never looked better.

The rating: PG, Pretty Gratifying. Harassment was by far the most popular trick in the book since it provided avengers with the most bang for their buck. **The curtain call:** Irresistibly safe and nasty at the same time. It's kind of like having wild sex with a Hell's Angel on his motorcycle—except he's wearing a condom and the bike isn't moving.

Act Three: Physical Damage

The method: Selective vandalizing: You make the box; you break the box. **The madness:** Whenever there's physical evidence of a crime, the chance of conviction increases dramatically. In other words, you break it, you could buy it. **The protagonist:** A person with destructive tendencies. She may fondly remember childhood Halloweens when she covered cars with shaving cream, hurl breakable objects in moments of rage, have a fascination for demolition derbies, or just be a big Jerry Lewis fan. **The staging:** Wreck and/or ruin of personal property was the main focus of this category. Many employees chose to attack their boss's sense of smell by strategically hiding garlic, eggs, fish oil, and raw meat around his or her office. One woman actually emptied her bowels on her manager's beloved antique desk. Krazy Glue antics were also popular: File drawers, desk chairs, office-door locks, and telephone receivers were favored sticky subjects. In the discard pile, lashers threw out important keys, erased computer files, and shredded crucial documents—in short, they took a stroll through Fawn Hall. **The players:**

• *Barbra, twenty-six, executive secretary.* My boss routinely humiliated me in public by making lewd comments at my expense. I finally reached my breaking point at an office party when he said in front of a group of men, "Hey, Barb, if you're not careful, your chest is going to pop right through your blouse. You know, they don't sew buttons on like they used to." They all laughed; I was mortified. A few days later, I crept into his office while he was out to lunch. On top of being rude beyond belief, he had a perspiration problem, so he kept a box of clean shirts in his bottom drawer. With a pair of scissors, I carefully snipped at the shirt buttons until every one was literally hanging by a thread. Then I stacked the shirts neatly, and put them back in place. Coincidentally, that afternoon, the chairman called a meeting. My boss had just returned from lunch, all sweaty and gross, and he bellowed at me to print out some reports while he changed his shirt. I stood by the printer and listened in delight to the string of curses as one by one, the buttons clattered to the floor. When he emerged from his office in his original shirt, drenched in sweat and frustration, I smiled sweetly, and said, "You know, you were right—they *don't* sew buttons on like they used to."

• *Libby, twenty-eight, computer technician.* The day my boss called me a birdbrain was the day I vowed to get even with her. I started searching for a job and, miraculously, in a couple of weeks, I got an offer. Then, I put my "birdbrained" plan in motion. On Saturday, my boyfriend and I drove out to the country, and got a pigeon from a woman who had a pigeon coop. That evening, I went to my boss's office, bird in hand—or rather, in box. I scattered a bunch of bread crumbs around, set out a few paper cups of water, then freed the pigeon, and quickly left, relocking the door behind me. My boss was on a business trip until Tuesday. When she opened her door, the pigeon—who'd had its fill of solitary confinement—flew out, madly flapping, into her face. She shrieked like a car alarm—people on other floors said they heard her. The room was a mess: Water spilled everywhere, papers in disarray, and bird poop galore. She took one look and started to cry. In the middle of her sobs, I walked in and said, "I want you to know that I'm going to another firm. I gave two weeks' notice to Personnel as of yesterday. By the way, I love what you've done with your office!" And walked out.

• *Donna, twenty-four, advertising executive.* My boss had a very expensive linen suit that he wore whenever he had an important luncheon or meeting to go to. On those mornings, he'd come in and fling the jacket at me, expecting me to hang it up for him. I would dutifully put it on a hanger, which was on a hook behind his door. Then, when he was in the bathroom, I'd put the jacket on the floor and bunch it up between the open door and the wall, making it look like it had fallen by accident. By the time his lunch rolled around, the jacket would be a mass of wrinkles. Although he'd yell, "Goddamnit, this always happens!" for some reason, he never suspected me. And even though it was a small thing, it always gave me joy to see him shuffling out of the building, looking like a crumpled wad of Kleenex.

• *Ramona, twenty-eight, pharmaceutical representative.* For a little over a year, I reported to a horrible woman who never had one kind word to say. She also had a weakness for chocolate. My friend had a pet rabbit, so one weekend, I gathered up fifty or so rabbit droppings and dipped them in melted chocolate. Then I wrapped them up in a pretty velvet box and sent them UPS to my boss, with a forged thank-you note from one of our clients. Naturally, when she got them, she immediately tore off the lid and started munching away. Toward the end of the afternoon, I walked into her office, just as she was popping the last "chocolate" into her mouth. I pretended not to notice and, instead, looked at the box, pointed, and gasped, "You got a box of those, too? They were sent all over the company! You didn't eat any, did you? Because I heard that some crazy guy has been dipping rabbit turds in chocolate and mailing them out . . ." I didn't have to continue because my boss interrupted me by puking—all over the desk and down the front of her. It was a wonderfully revolting sight to behold.

The rating: R, Risky and Rude, but on some levels, Really tempting. It seems that inside many members of the work force, there's a tiny juvenile delinquent screaming to get out. **The curtain call:** The odds of being nabbed are a mite too high for us; plus, we don't really cotton to the pillage-and-plunder approach. Even if the damage is trivial, and no one gets hurt, we don't love the concept. Then again, we never liked Jerry Lewis, either.

Act Four: Humiliation

The method: Degradation, abasement, mockery: Essentially, you do unto your boss as she has done unto you. **The madness:** Humiliation plots can be complicated and usually require more calculation than other revenge methods. Hence, the margin of error is bigger—but, according to our humiliators, so is the margin of return. **The protagonist:** Anyone who has a particularly sadistic boss and/or a well-cultivated mean streak. **The staging:** Like snowflakes, no two low blows were exactly alike—each woman had her own highly original way of reducing her victim to silt. For them, iniquity was the mother of invention. **The players:**

- *Polly, twenty-seven, public relations account executive.* I'd spent two years making coffee and copies before I got promoted from assistant to account executive. I was thrilled—but it didn't last long. My boss's new assistant turned out to be a real dud. She got fired within four weeks, and who replaced her in the interim? Me. After a while, I noticed that my boss wasn't even interviewing people; when I asked her why, she said I was doing so well, she didn't see the point of spending the money on another assistant. In other words, I'd been demoted. Furious, I plotted revenge. My boss was going to be a bridesmaid at her younger sister's wedding and had been dieting like crazy—probably so she wouldn't look like a fat old maid. Since I fetched her lunches for her, I started getting the most fattening muffins, soups, and salad dressings, all the while assuring her that they were low- to no-fat. I put sugar and cream in her coffee instead of skim milk and NutraSweet; I gave her real ice cream in place of Skimpy Treat. When she started to gain weight, she joined a high-priced health club— and only ended up going a couple of times. On the day of the wedding, she was fifteen pounds heavier than when she'd started. I heard her telling someone on the phone that her dress fitting was the most humiliating experience of her life. After that, whenever she put me down, I just imagined her looking like a giant pink taffeta gumball and laughed.

- *Alyssa, twenty-eight, music agent.* I was the only woman on a staff of male chauvinists—and my boss Steve was the worst. He did everything he could to purposely exclude me. Eventually, he ended up pushing me out. A few months later, I was reading a gossip column, when I saw a picture of him posing with the

Rolling Stones. It set me off. He had such a smug look on his face, I wanted to puncture his pompous male ego, expose him as a fool. So I came up with a scheme: I had a girlfriend call up my replacement (who was new and didn't really know what he was doing) and say, "Hi, this is Suzy from Virgin Records! I'm calling on behalf of Mick and Keith. They had such fun with Steve the other night, they'd like to invite him and his entire staff to a private party at Spago, this Friday night. Steve's name will be on the list at the door, and he's allowed to bring fifteen guests. If there's a problem, just tell him to say he's friends with Mick, okay? Great—see ya there!" The next Monday, I found out what happened from the office receptionist. She told me that Steve had bragged about the invitation far and wide and made a big deal over picking whom he would take with him. When he and his flunkies showed up at Spago, the maître d' refused to let him in. True to form, Steve threw a fit, proclaiming he was "Mick Jagger's close personal friend" and made a complete ass of himself in front of all the people in the restaurant—many of whom had professional relationships with him. Finally, they kicked him out in utter ignominy. It was everything I'd ever hoped for.

- *Melanie, twenty-six, copy editor.* Our department was run by a copy chief who was universally despised. She was in her late thirties, single, and resentful as hell about it. She was so unrelentingly caustic, it was impossible to feel at all sympathetic towards her. The last straw was when she made us come in to work on New Year's Eve. One of the editors had a boyfriend flying in from Switzerland and tried to beg off, but our boss said she could either come in or consider herself unemployed. I mean, can you believe? Our New Year's resolution that year: To make our boss pay for her evil ways. We chipped in and secretly hired a gorgeous guy from an escort service to pick her up in a bar and sweet-talk the living pants off her. Literally. He had strict instructions not to tell her he was a hired hand—so to speak. Being a lonely woman, she fell madly in love with him; every day, she waited for him to call. He didn't, obviously. After a week, we left a phone message on her desk with the guy's name and the escort service's number. In a tizzy, she called up and asked for him. Her assistant told us that, when he got on the line, she identified herself, and for a few minutes, he couldn't even remember who she was. Then, he must have revealed what he did for a living because she started saying, "What? Who hired you? You were only saying those things because of the money?" Thankfully, he never identified us, saving us from an early death. In the end, she threw the phone across the room and slammed her door shut for the rest of the afternoon. We had a few initial pangs, but the next day, when she fired an assistant for getting her a regular soda instead of diet, we knew she'd gotten exactly what she deserved.

The rating: NC-17, No Comment (that's the 17th Amendment, right?). A girl either goes for this nasty little genre, or she doesn't. **The curtain call:** Truth be told, the victors in this category expressed more visceral satisfaction than any of their sisters in crime. Nevertheless, we're torn: While we think the story about the Rolling Stones party is a gas, the other tales are too rich (rhymes with witch) for our blood. But it's your bile-game—you make the call.

Act Five: Professional Sabotage

The method: You fiddle such that Rome burns. **The madness:** Medium to high. If you're only trying to put chinks in your boss's reputation, anonymity is possible. But if you're trying to topple an entire career empire, you may have to identify yourself—and possibly suffer the consequences. **The protagonist:** A hireling who's been so trampled, she has nothing (more) to lose. **The staging:** Most secondary offenses were committed electronically. Some saboteurs sent damaging E-mail from their bosses' computers; others (who worked at companies where telephone calls were monitored) secretly racked up long-distance hours on their managers' phones. A few left fake, incriminating phone messages—with implications of job hunting, adultery, tax evasion, or alcoholism—at the receptionist's desk for all to see. Similarly, false faxes were also transmitted (usually by friends in cahoots) with the same intent to publicly damn. With first-degree offenders, though, the stakes shot up drastically. So much so that none of our big-time underminers would agree to attribution. We don't blame them. **The players:**

- A woman who worked for a corporation with large government contracts discovered her boss was skimming money from the company. Over the course of several years, he pocketed $23 million. When he fired her with unjust cause, she let his scam out of the bag. For her whistle-blowing efforts, she was handsomely rewarded—to the tune of $11 million.
- One retail manager's boss (the corporate CEO) was legendary for his bad management skills, not to

mention his rampant infidelity. The third time he passed her over for a promotion, she secretly raided his office for evidence of his adultery (phone messages, personal notes, photographs, credit-card receipts), put them in an envelope, and anonymously mailed them to his wife. Did we mention that his wife owned the company? Needless to say, this cheater didn't prosper—he was summarily divorced and dismissed.

- A restaurant employee had been groped by her boss one time too many. When she protested, he fired her. To get even, she informed the authorities of his questionable hiring procedures (illegal aliens paid under the table) and his creative bookkeeping (one set of books for the IRS, another for himself). He lost his grill—and ended up behind bars.

The rating: X—as in Xerox your résumé if you intend to play in the majors. When you take official steps to bring your boss down, there's a good chance you'll have to bow out in the process. Preferably, you'll have left the scene before you commit/expose the crime (ideally, you'll also have another job lined up: Prospective employers are reluctant to hire a known whistle blower, no matter how justified her actions may have been). **The verdict:** Minor sabotage is comparable to harassment—pure mischief with an attractive tinge of malice. High-grade subversion is a horse of a different choler, though—so think long and hard before you set your scar date.

Which brings us to the end of our five acts. But don't touch that dial: Skimming through the script doesn't automatically make you qualified to perform. Not that you'd ever dream of doing such a thing. Still, just in case you have a "friend" who would, we thought we'd review a few rules of last resort. For starters, keep it simple. Complex guerrilla strategies are the terrain of pimply military wonks. Too many details spoil the revenge broth—on occasion, they can even tip the whole pot over.

Next, keep it legal. Think disgruntled postal workers. Think Amy Fisher. Does the world really need any more rag-hag miniseries? Noop. Which is why you'll take pains to stay within the legal pale. Legal means you don't inflict physical injury (assault, battery), you don't make death threats or call in bomb scares (intimidation, harmful intent), you don't break into the office and steal anything (forcible entry, theft), and you don't wave sharp objects or firearms about (illegal possession of a weapon). Most important, if you plan to let your fingers do the stalking, you make damn sure your boss doesn't have Caller I.D. at home (ass coverage).

Thirdly, keep it to yourself. Limit outside involvement to a bare minimum—the more accomplices there are, the less damage control you have. Furthermore, a good little avenger determines beforehand whether her actions will affect those around her. This is trickier than it sounds. Revenge has a nasty habit of producing unexpected fallout. At worst, you flick that front domino over, a crazy chain reaction ensues, and before you can say "Tonya made me do it," your boyfriend auctions off your home movies, some snippy chick is limping around Disneyland, and you're turning triple-toe loops in a six-by-nine cell. At best, the aftershocks merely leave you dazed and confused, scratching your head, wondering—

Ellen: What fresh hell is this?
Val: That's for sure. When it came to revenge, our per-

fect crime skipped from ordinary harassment to humiliation to borderline sabotage, like Bob Dylan on vinyl.

E: Would you care to elaborate?

V: Gladly. Born Robert Zimmerman in 1941, Bob Dylan would soon become one of the most important rock influences of his . . .

E: Hold it, Casey Kasem. Not that part, the revenge part.

V: Oh. Let's see . . . how should I set this up? It was early October, about six months after your stormy exit. You were living in Chicago; I was still in the office, being gouged by Roz. It was awful—I used to call you every morning, and say, "I'm not sure if I can make it until five o'clock."

E: The despair in your voice made my heart sink. Then, one miraculous morning, you sounded different. You sounded almost . . . happy. You said—

V: "Something's happening here, and it's big."

E: Really big.

V: Huge. Roz's boss, Leslie, had been fired, and the whole department was being turned over. To be fair, we were sorry to see Leslie leave—apart from buying Roz's suck-up act, she'd always been nice to us. Nonetheless, her departure gave us a glimmer of hope. That Roz would be the next to go.

E: A week later, Claire, the new editor-in-chief, was officially sworn in. The morning you met her, you called me up, giddy as a gin fizz, and exclaimed—

V: "She's so great! She's smart, pretty, and—get this— she looked me in the eye and *smiled* at me!" It's sad, but back then, eye contact and friendly facial expressions were rare commodities.

E: Overnight, you renewed your lease on life. Apathy transformed to energy. You started working at full speed, churning out story ideas like a, well, like a full-speed story-idea churn. And your efforts were rewarded. Claire recognized you as an asset; furthermore, she saw Roz as a liability. When November came, we were given true cause for thanks: Before Roz could even start her Ghost of Christmas Sucks routine, she got axed.

V: Dinged.

E: Donged. The witch was dead; we were jubilant. For a while, every day was cause for celebration. Then, out of nowhere, you developed a strange hankering for—

V: Just desserts. Mind you, I'm usually the least vindictive person. But I'd heard through the rumor mill that when Roz was packing up her office, she pocketed a book of car-service vouchers. She bragged to a mutual acquaintance that she'd called a car to take her from Manhattan to New Jersey, in a blinding snowstorm, so she could go to the outlet malls. She even made the car wait three hours for her and drive her home. For some reason, this incensed me. I thought, "That woman just continues to rape this company for all its worth. I'm busting my butt; meanwhile, she's feeding off my labor, spending money I helped earn on interstate shopping sprees. Dammit, I'm still working for her! Who does she think she is?" I phoned you up in a blind fury. When you answered, I said—

E: "She must be stopped. *She. Must. Be. Stopped.*" Your voice was so strangled, I couldn't figure out who you were for a second. You explained the situation and ranted something about how you wanted to starve the parasite.

V: Fleece the goat.

E: Spank the monkey. You were intent on staging a

crackdown—and you asked for my help. After some consideration, I decided, "How could I possibly refuse my dear pal Val?" Translation: How could I possibly resist?

V: The plot unfolded. First, we set a few parameters. We agreed to limit ourselves strictly to work-related revenge; it wasn't fair to make Roz feel personally scared or threatened. Next, we drew up a letter of intent: We would attempt to prevent Roz from having any pleasure at the company's expense. This meant finding a way to confiscate her car privileges. While we told ourselves we were nobly saving corporate dollars, in truth, we were equally interested in kicking Roz off the gravy train. She'd treated us like mud for years—let her eat dirt.

E: The plot thickened. Claire was French, but she'd lived in Zurich for several years—her immediate distinguishing trait was a lilting Swiss-French accent. Incredibly, I'd made a friend in Chicago named Ilsa who had the *exact* same accent; her voice was so dead-on Claire, it was uncanny. Clearly, she had been sent to us by the revenge gods. The plan was simple: Pretending to be Claire, Ilsa would leave a message on Roz's answering machine, and bust her on the car voucher scam. As a test run, I had Ilsa call *you* up and say, "Hello, Valerie? Claire, here. Word has it that you intend to play a little joke on Roz, and I must say I find it rather amusing." Your reaction was awesome: After a good thirty-second pause, you practically screamed—

V: "WHAT???" I tell you, I died a thousand deaths. I fell for it, hook, line, and sinker. It wasn't until I heard you guys laughing that I realized I'd been duped. I didn't care. Because as I waited for my heart rate to slow down, one thought rang in my head, over and over: *This harebrained scheme could actually work.*

E: We decided to place our call right before Roz was meeting two people from the office for drinks. The idea was that she'd pick up the message, freak out and tell them about it, and then they'd blab about it to us. This way, we could find out if we'd succeeded and, if so, gauge our force of impact.

V: Rate of return.

E: Proof of purchase. At three P.M. on the fateful day, Ilsa dialed Roz's number. She got the answering machine and left the following message: "Roz, it's Claire. We understand that you've been using company car vouchers for personal purposes. Since you're no longer an employee of the company, you'll be expected to cover the outstanding charges. You should be receiving a bill shortly, okay? Thanks." Having cast our stone, we waited for the report.

V: It was a short wait. The very next morning, I ran into one of Roz's drinking companions—we'll call her G. for grapevine—on the subway. As predicted, G. could barely wait to dish. Brimming with excitement, she informed me that Claire had called Roz the previous afternoon. Since Roz was in the bathtub—why she was taking a bath at three P.M., we'll never know—she let the machine pick up. The way Roz told it, when she heard a French-Swiss accent on her tape, she wrapped herself up in a towel and climbed out, just in time to hear "Claire" bark, "Look, we know you're using company car vouchers, and you're going to pay!" I smiled, and thought, "Not exactly, but close enough." G. added that Roz was visibly rattled and angered by the experience. I repressed the urge to dance a hornpipe and murmured, "Really? That's interesting."

E: The second you got to the office, you phoned me and relayed the news of our crowning triumph. We congratulated each other a few hundred times, thrilling to the notion that we'd actually pulled it off. Our mission had been accomplished.

V: Unfortunately, it was the accomplishment that kept on accomplishing. You see, we hadn't quite bargained on G. recounting the episode to our managing editor, who told Claire, who, of course, denied everything. The plot unraveled. The managing editor saw this as proof that Roz was a crook and a liar who was unilaterally intent on destroying Claire; she had Roz banned from the building. In no time, the tale spread like brush fire, getting taller with each retelling. In one version, Claire threatened Roz with litigation. In another, they'd had a face-to-face confrontation. The craziest permutation involved a car being hot-wired. We sat helplessly as account after skewed account came back to us—it was like a giant game of Telephone, spun out of control.

E: What's worse, months later, we discovered that we'd inadvertently sparked off a false alarm. Apparently, there were other voucher vultures in the company who, upon hearing the story, were now living in fear of being nabbed. The accounting department must have wondered about the sudden dip in car expenses. Unintentionally, our isolated hit ended up affecting people we didn't even know.

V: Luckily, despite the slight error in judgment, no real harm was done. In fact, last week, I called Claire and confessed—I wanted to get her permission before we made a full public disclosure. She just laughed and said, "Brilliant! You did some good."

E: She did? That makes me feel better. Still, you have to admit, our petty revenge efforts turned out to be gratuitous. In the excitement, we forgot about one incontrovertible element of fate: Karmic justice. Ultimately, we should have realized that, regardless of our shenanigans, Roz would inevitably get her due.

V: And then some. After a long, dry spell of unemployment, Roz landed a mediocre job, only to be fired within six months. Since then, she's pretty much faded into obscurity. In the interim, you went to work at another magazine where, glory be, you were graced with a terrific boss—

E: —while you got a great boss of your own and a promotion to boot. So we pulled through okay, don't you think, Val? And now, here we are, together again—a pair of older, hopefully wiser, partners in crime.

V: Comrades in arms.

E: Friends to the finish.

Which, conveniently, is where we are right now. It's been an awfully grueling eight hours—shouldn't you be heading home? Before you leave, though, consider this: At the end of the day, lashing back isn't nearly as important as moving forward. Because the best things in life have nothing to do with paybacks or power plays. The rat race is for people like your boss, who need to keep running in circles. Let them run. You know where you live.

Marshall Sella

About the Authors

ELLEN TIEN graduated from Vassar College and was a senior editor at *Mademoiselle* and *Cosmopolitan* magazines. VALERIE FRANKEL graduated from Dartmouth College and is the author of four mystery novels (including *Prime Time for Murder* and *A Body to Die For*). They met at *Mademoiselle*, where Ellen is currently a contributing editor, and Val, a senior editor. Their first book together was *The Heartbreak Handbook*. They both live and work in New York City.